THE AMAZING JOKE BOOK

THE AMAZING JOKE BOOK

THE ULTIMATE COLLECTION OF HILARIOUS ONE-LINERS, PUNS AND GAGS

JOEL AND JOHN JESSUP

All images: Shutterstock

This edition published in 2019 by Arcturus Publishing Limited
26/27 Bickels Yard, 151–153 Bermondsey Street,
London SE1 3HA

AD006637UK

Printed in the UK

Contents

Introduction

What makes a good joke?

Sometimes it's a pun or a play on words. Sometimes it's a shaggy dog story or a logic that's pushed to an absurd extreme. Whatever it is that makes you laugh, you'll find it on these pages. Here are hundreds of jokes on all subjects, from the familiar (office politics) to the unexpected (quantum physics). Here too is Shakespeare struggling to buy a drink. Here are the frustrations of modern life, and of life after the apocalypse. From the A of alcohol to the X, Y, Z of xylophones, yetis and zombies, there's a joke here for everyone.

Alcohol

Arial and Times New Roman walk into a bar. The barman takes one look at them and says, "Sorry, fellas, we don't serve your type in here."

★ ☆ ★ ☆ ★ ☆ ★ ☆ ★ ☆ ★ ☆ ★

Two drunks in a bar are having a slurred conversation.

"I'm most happy," says the first, "when I've had ten pints of lager, three gin and tonics and five glasses of scotch whisky."

"I'm most happy," replies the second, "when I've had sixteen highballs, two martinis on the rocks, four glasses of absinthe, a bottle of Merlot and a packet of dry-roasted peanuts."

The first drunk pulls a face: "Oh no, that'd be too much for me. Dry-roasted peanuts? I can never eat on a full stomach."

I went to Cuba and my girlfriend asked me to send her a photo of me drinking in a bar that Hemingway drank in. I went one better and found a bar that he didn't drink in!

A piece of straight, clean string goes into a bar and orders a gin and tonic. The barman serves the drink, the string downs it and walks out.

Ten minutes later a dirty, twisted, ragged piece of string walks into the bar. "Are you that piece of string that was here ten minutes ago?" asks the barman.

"No," replies the string, "I'm a frayed knot."

An atom walks into a bar and asks the man behind the counter if he's seen his missing electron. "Are you sure she's missing?" asks the bartender.
"I'm positive," replies the atom.

Two women are moving into a new flat. They've put the furniture in place, cleaned and tidied and unpacked all their stuff. The first woman then says to the second, "You should go out and get some supplies. I saw a shop around the corner." The second woman nods before heading off. Thirty minutes later she returns with five cases of Chardonnay and a loaf of bread.

"What's this?" The first woman stares in disbelief. "Are we having a party or something?"

"No," comes the reply.

"Then what did you buy all that bread for?"

James Bond walks into a cocktail lounge and goes up to the barman. "I'll have a vodka martini, stirred, not shaken," he requests.

The barman looks at him: "Are you sure, sir? It's normally the other way round."

Mr Bond replies, "Well, I'm on holiday."

> The derivation of the word *whisky* comes from the old Irish *uisce beatha*, or water of life. So why is it you wake up in the morning feeling like death?

An iron and a hat walk into a pub. The hat walks up to the bar and orders two beers. The bartender refuses: "I'm sorry, there's no way I can serve you two."

"Why not?" asks the hat.

"Because you're off your head and your mate's steaming."

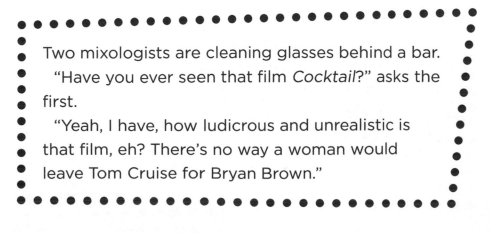

Two mixologists are cleaning glasses behind a bar.

"Have you ever seen that film *Cocktail*?" asks the first.

"Yeah, I have, how ludicrous and unrealistic is that film, eh? There's no way a woman would leave Tom Cruise for Bryan Brown."

A man walks into a bar and says to the bartender, "I bet I can get you to give me a free drink." Intrigued, the bartender asks him how he plans to do that.

"If I can get you to say no," the man says, "you have to give me a free drink, okay?"

"You're on!" replies the barman.

"Right," says the man, "give me a free drink!"

The bartender shakes his head: "You must think I'm really stupid."

"What, have you heard this one before?" the man asks.

Surprised, the bartender replies, "No... oh, damn, I said it!" He grudgingly serves the man a glass of scotch. "Alright, you can have this one," he tells the man angrily, "but as soon as you're finished you can get out – you're barred for life!" The man shrugs, chugs his drink and leaves.

The next night the same man walks into the bar. The bartender regards him grimly: "I told you that you were barred."

"I'm sorry, we've never met before, this is my first time in here," says the man with genuine surprise and feeling.

The bartender is taken aback. "Well, then, you must have a double."

"Thanks very much," the man says. "Make it a scotch!"

* * * * ★ ★ ★ ★ ★ * * *

Shakespeare walks into a pub. The bartender says, "Get out, you're bard!"

* * * * ★ ★ ★ ★ * * *

Five women looking for a new place for a night out stumble across a mysterious bar they've never seen before. As they enter, they see the place is completely empty except for a cloaked figure behind the counter. They sit down and ask what's available. "Every cocktail you can imagine!" the figure says. "But be careful what you choose."

The first lady orders a grasshopper, and she's amazed that after finishing the glass it transforms into a real grasshopper and leaps out of her hand.

The second lady, meanwhile, orders a white Russian; once she's done, Rasputin appears, takes the glass from her hand and fixes her with his terrible stare. The third lady orders a hurricane and the room is suddenly battered by a very high blustery wind.

The fourth woman looks in alarm at the others because she's ordered an old fashioned and suddenly finds herself dressed as someone from the nineteenth century, complete with very tight corset. She suddenly starts laughing hysterically.

"What's so funny?" asks her friend.

"Well, you just ordered a horse's neck!"

Two friends visit a whisky distillery. As they come to the end of the tour, they are greeted by a massive vault filled with oak casks. The guide smiles and says to them, "These casks are not full because over the years at least 10 per cent of the whisky evaporates during the process of fermentation. We call this 'The Angel's Share'."

Everyone in the group laughs except for one of the friends. On their way out he grabs his companion: "Right, here's the plan," he says. "Get down to the fancy dress shop. We need halos, wings and a couple of harps."

Two rich people are on an exclusive holiday in the wine region of California. One says to the other: "You know, Eleanor, I don't think much of this treading grapes! This is the third pair of Louboutins I've ruined today!"

There's a man in a pub drinking tequila even though there's a three-for-one deal on beers. The man next to him is curious why he didn't go for the special offer.

"Oh, I have a strict drinking regime," he says. "I only drink mojitos on Mondays, Tuesday is only Tom Collins, Wednesdays is wheat beer, Thursdays – as you see – I only drink tequila, Fridays are French white wine, and Saturdays are Singapore slings."

"Wow. What do you have on Sunday?"

"An appointment at a rehab clinic."

Aliens

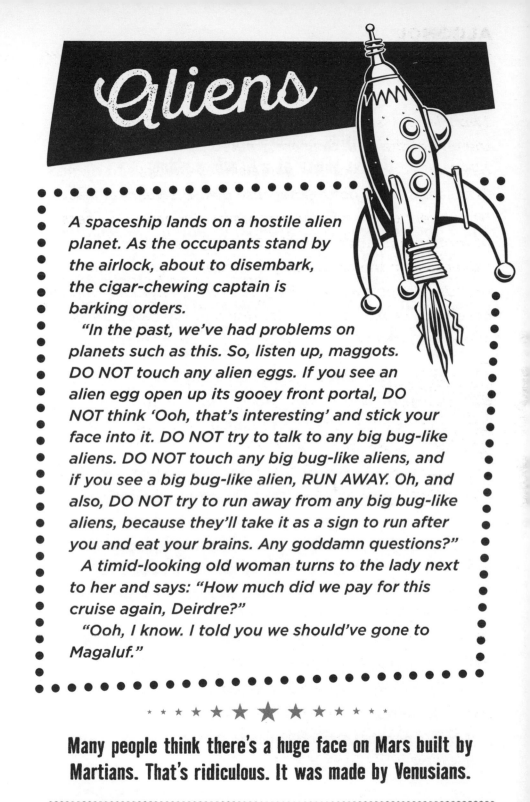

A spaceship lands on a hostile alien planet. As the occupants stand by the airlock, about to disembark, the cigar-chewing captain is barking orders.

"In the past, we've had problems on planets such as this. So, listen up, maggots. DO NOT touch any alien eggs. If you see an alien egg open up its gooey front portal, DO NOT think 'Ooh, that's interesting' and stick your face into it. DO NOT try to talk to any big bug-like aliens. DO NOT touch any big bug-like aliens, and if you see a big bug-like alien, RUN AWAY. Oh, and also, DO NOT try to run away from any big bug-like aliens, because they'll take it as a sign to run after you and eat your brains. Any goddamn questions?"

A timid-looking old woman turns to the lady next to her and says: "How much did we pay for this cruise again, Deirdre?"

"Ooh, I know. I told you we should've gone to Magaluf."

Many people think there's a huge face on Mars built by Martians. That's ridiculous. It was made by Venusians.

Flying saucers aren't real.
Unless you're at a Greek wedding.

The eighteenth-century astronomer Giovanni Schiaparelli had just installed a brand-new, top-of-the-range telescope in his observatory and sat down to focus it on Mars, which was especially visible at that time of year.

Suddenly he leaped back, his face full of surprise. "My god... canals! I can't believe it! Mars is covered in canals!"

He ran from his place to find his friend and fellow astronomer Angelo. "I can't believe it, there are canals on Mars!" he announced to his colleague breathlessly. "Evidence of intelligent life!"

"Calm down, my friend," said Angelo, patting him kindly. "You have just installed a new telescope. Perhaps it is streaks on the lens, or a problem with the alignment."

"You are right, my friend," replied Giovanni soberly. They returned to his observatory and proceeded to carefully clean the biggest lens and test the alignment of all the others.

Sitting down once again, he looked through the eye piece. He then sat back, a dour look on his face.

"What is it, Giovanni?" said Angelo sympathetically. "No canals anymore?"

"No, it's not that," said Giovanni. "That guy's gondola just sank!"

Peaceful aliens come to Earth and share their technology with us, but with various caveats.

One of the technologies they bring is teleportation, enabling people to be instantly transported from one side of the planet to the other. The first ever human volunteer for this technique walks up to the portal and is greeted by the alien attendant.

"Now, human, there is one thing you must know. When you pass into the portal all the atoms in your body will be converted to energy."

"Right."

"This energy will then be sent across the planet at the speed of light, and then matter at the other side will be reassembled using the information. It will construct a copy of you. This other you may look like you, talk like you, even think like you. But we cannot guarantee how it will behave, or what it will do. The travel may have distorted it somehow. There is a small chance it may even be a cruel, destructive monster, for whose behaviour you are responsible!"

The volunteer stepped back.

"In that case I think I'll give it a miss, mate. If I wanted that, I'd have had children!"

★ ★

People who think they've been abducted by aliens always claim they've been captured, taken to a big white room and then probed. It sounds more like they're actually being taken to the vet.

Allergies

A man goes to his doctor and says, "I've got an allergy to something. My nose is so stuffed up it makes a whistling noise every time I breathe, listen...."

And as the man breathes through his nose the doctor can hear a sound like "Hoo! Hoo! Hoo!"

The man stops. "So, what do you think the problem is?"

The doctor thinks, then shrugs. "Hoo nose?"

The boy in the bubble was so allergic he had to be protected in quarantine. He had to face isolation, loneliness and, perhaps worst of all, Paul Simon writing a weird song about him.

I told my wife I was allergic to housework, to which she said: "I want a divorce." It's not very funny but it is what actually happened.

● ● ● ● ● ● ● ● ● ● ● ● ● ● ● ● ●

When asked on the street whether they'd rather be allergic to chocolate or champagne, 85% of people chose to punch the person conducting the survey.

> Nomophobia is the fear of losing cellphone coverage. Presumably because you have No mo phone to use.

Allergies can sometimes cause shortness of breath. Genetics can cause shortness of person. Modern life can cause shortness of money. Scottish people make shortbread.

★ ★ ★ ★ ★ ★ ★ ★ ★ ★ ★

It seems like everyone nowadays has a nut allergy. Every time I nut someone they come out in lumps.

Two young women are talking. One says, "I went to the doctor yesterday about my nut allergy, and he gave me this EpiPen!"

"Ooh," says the second. "I hope you don't have to use it."

"I already have!" says the first. "But it didn't fill out my crossword very well."

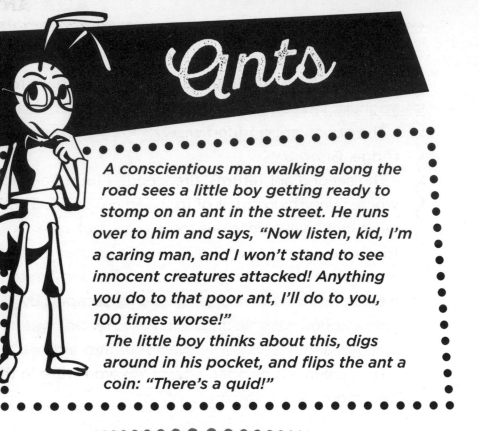

Ants

A conscientious man walking along the road sees a little boy getting ready to stomp on an ant in the street. He runs over to him and says, "Now listen, kid, I'm a caring man, and I won't stand to see innocent creatures attacked! Anything you do to that poor ant, I'll do to you, 100 times worse!"

The little boy thinks about this, digs around in his pocket, and flips the ant a coin: "There's a quid!"

Why do ants rarely get sick?
Because they have anty-bodies.

An ant colony is desperate for food, so they decide to send three ants out to the nearest house to see if they can find anything they can eat.

The first ant returns, shivering, and says, "Well, I found a massive white monolith. When a human pulled at the front of it, a great light shone out! I managed to get inside and it was full of fresh cheese and milk and meat, but it was all really cold and too big, so I couldn't bring any of it back. When it closed, it was pitch-black. I only managed to escape by waiting for it to open again and clinging on to a yoghurt. I'm sorry."

The queen ant nodded wisely: "Ah, you were in a fridge. Good try."

The second ant returns, drenched: "I found a place where everything smelt of fruit and it was filled with what looked like delicious food items, but when I tried one it tasted awful, like chemicals, and made my stomach hurt. Suddenly a human came and started a rain shower and I had to run! I only escaped by jumping down a hole and riding a torrent of water through a pipe and out of the house into a drain."

The queen ant nodded again: "Ah, you were in the bathroom. A worthy attempt."

The third ant returns, looking even more dishevelled than the other two: "Well, I had a real adventure. I was on the living room carpet, looking for particles of food, when suddenly this enormous snorting noise assailed me and I was sucked up into a massive dark hole! Then I found myself in this warm place with no light at all, like a big bag, and it was completely full of particles of food and bits of dust – a perfect larder for us!"

The ant queen nodded. "Ah, you were in a vacuum cleaner. But tell me, how did you escape?"

"Well," the third replied, "at some point they took the vacuum cleaner out for a walk and I came out with a massive crap that it did on the pavement."

ANTS

A huge group of ants are walking along, looking for food for their colony, but they can't seem to find anything. When they finally come across a single morsel of stale food, they begin to fight over who will have the honour of carrying this single piece of nourishment back to their queen. It looks like turning into a bloodbath until suddenly an ant that none of them had seen before comes forward. The other ants fall silent and watch in wonder as the newcomer takes the single piece of food and manages to hand each one of the ants its own piece of food to take back to the colony. It then walks away in silence, seemingly satisfied.

"Who was that?!" asks one of the ants.

"Don't you know?" says another. "That was the Anty Christ."

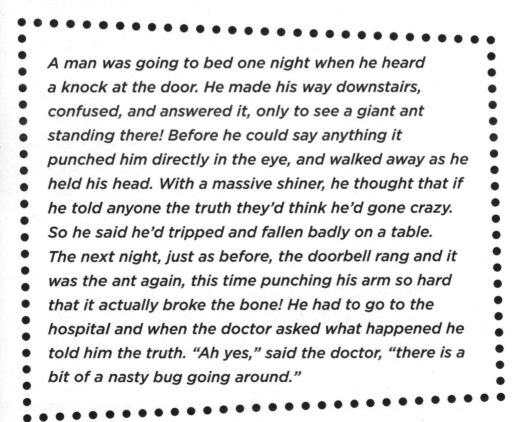

A man was going to bed one night when he heard a knock at the door. He made his way downstairs, confused, and answered it, only to see a giant ant standing there! Before he could say anything it punched him directly in the eye, and walked away as he held his head. With a massive shiner, he thought that if he told anyone the truth they'd think he'd gone crazy. So he said he'd tripped and fallen badly on a table. The next night, just as before, the doorbell rang and it was the ant again, this time punching his arm so hard that it actually broke the bone! He had to go to the hospital and when the doctor asked what happened he told him the truth. "Ah yes," said the doctor, "there is a bit of a nasty bug going around."

One ant comes over to another and asks, "Hey, have you seen Reg around?"

"No," the other ant replies, "I don't know Reg. What does he look like?"

"Well, he's got a shiny black carapace, two big buggy eyes, prehensile jaws..."

"That describes all of us, you need to be more specific!"

The first ant thinks. "OK, he's got six legs, he can lift 100 times his own weight..."

"No, that still describes all of us! Try again."

The first ant thinks again. "OK. He wears a tiny Argyle sweater, a little pair of corduroy trousers and three pairs of purple suede loafers."

The second ant pauses. "Ah, okay, he's just over here!" He takes him over to an ant wearing a tiny Argyle sweater, a little pair of corduroy trousers and three pairs of purple suede loafers.

"That's not Reg, that's Martin," the first ant declares.

"Really?!" says the second ant. "What are the chances of there being two ants in this world with a tiny Argyle sweater, a little pair of corduroy trousers and three pairs of purple suede loafers!"

And then Martin pipes up: "Has Reg been in my wardrobe again?!"

* * * ★ ★ ★ ★ ★ * * *

How many ants do you need to fill a block of flats?
Ten ants.

* * * ★ ★ ★ ★ ★ * * *

Art

How many surrealists does it take to change a lightbulb? A fish.

* * * * * ★ ★ ★ ★ ★ * * *

Matisse, Picasso and Edward Hopper are sitting at the top of a cliff, enjoying the view. Suddenly a gust of wind blows all three of them over the edge.

As they plummet towards the ground, Matisse says, "Though this cliff seems barren, there are always flowers for those who want to see them."

Picasso says, "To me, the colours in this cliff, like the features of my face, follow the changes of my emotions."

And Edward Hopper says, "AAAAAGGGHHHHHHHHHH!!!!!!!!!!"

The most expensive painting in the world was sold for $450 million! Some people just love dogs playing poker.

Leonardo Da Vinci, apart from being an artist, was also an inventor and created the first scuba gear. Which is why his watercolours were a bit of a washout.

The Mona Lisa *was briefly kept in the bathroom of King Francis I. If you find that horrifying, you really don't want to know why the Venus de Milo doesn't have any arms.*

They say that there's an artist in everyone. All you need are the right tools, the right connections, and a lazy sausage dog.

In the basement of the Louvre, a famous art historian has summoned his closest peer.

"This is amazing news, Jacques! In Italy they were completing excavations near the old site of Leonardo da Vinci's workshop. They found a canvas buried in rock... which by its frame and age seems to be a counterpart painting to the *Mona Lisa* itself."

His friend was astonished. "Surely not!"

"It's true! Apparently the *Mona Lisa* is actually part of a diptych, two paintings acting as one. This painting is meant to be placed directly below *La Gioconda*. Perhaps it reveals why she is smiling. First, we must remove centuries of dust and grime."

And so, they carefully cleaned it, inch by inch, until finally they stepped back to see the true image...

The blushing art historian grabbed the painting and immediately threw it into an open furnace.

"I think we'll, um... keep this one to ourselves, eh, Jacques?"

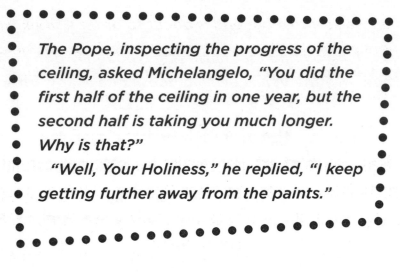

The Pope, inspecting the progress of the ceiling, asked Michelangelo, "You did the first half of the ceiling in one year, but the second half is taking you much longer. Why is that?"

"Well, Your Holiness," he replied, "I keep getting further away from the paints."

★ ★ ★ ★ ★ ★ ★ ★ ★ ★ ★ ★ ★ ★ ★ ★

While many talk about the apple that supposedly landed on Isaac Newton's head, not as many people know about the sausage dog that Jackson Pollock tripped over while carrying his paints. (Mr Littlelegs was later heard to say, "I prefer Rothko anyway.")

★ ★ ★ ★ ★ ★ ★ ★ ★ ★ ★ ★ ★ ★ ★ ★

> **Why did Michelangelo paint the Sistine ceiling on his back? Because if he'd painted it on his front it would've been called the Sistine floor.**

Some famous design schools are Art Nouveau, Art Deco, and Art Garfunkel – the last one known for its bridge over troubled water and paintings in the hazy shade of winter.

A man walks into a bar and is about to order a drink when he notices Vincent Van Gogh playing the fruit machine. "Hey, Van Gogh!" he calls over to him, "Want a drink?" Van Gogh replies, "No thanks. I've got one 'ere."

★ ★ ★ ★ ★ ★ **★** ★ ★ ★ ★ ★ ★

Many works of art now require painstakingly careful restoration to preserve them. One suggestion of using "a huge jar of vinegar" was rejected by everyone. Except Damian Hirst.

★ ★ ★ ★ ★ ★ **★** ★ ★ ★ ★ ★ ★

Tracy Emin submitted a replica of her unmade bed as a work of art. It was only once she submitted her wardrobe and her dressing table to the same gallery that they realised she was trying to move in.

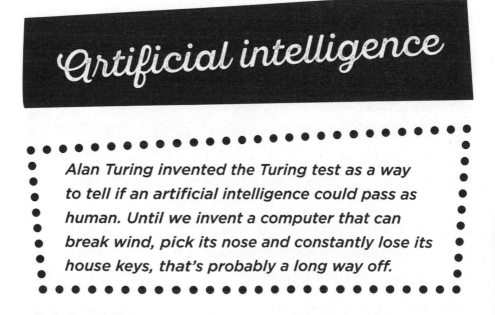

Artificial intelligence

Alan Turing invented the Turing test as a way to tell if an artificial intelligence could pass as human. Until we invent a computer that can break wind, pick its nose and constantly lose its house keys, that's probably a long way off.

★ ★

In 1996 IBM's artificial intelligence Deep Blue lost to Russian chess grandmaster Gary Kasparov. Then they tried chess.

In a fashionable local café, the grizzled-looking owner has installed a new coffee machine.

"Check out this thing," he muttered. "It's got this artificial intelligence installed, which controls the level of beans to water, how frothy the milk is, all the pressure settings!"

Then he indicates a nearby panel.

"And not just that. Apparently, if you stick your face here, it scans it and then gives you exactly what it thinks you need."

"Wow, let me try!" says his head barista, putting her face up against the scan plate. Two minutes later, the machine dispenses a hazelnut macchiato with soy foam.

"That is perfect," she says, sipping it. "But have you tried it?"

"Not yet," the owner says, shuffling over and sticking his face up against the plate.

The machine rumbles and judders for about 15 minutes... before spitting out a comb and a voucher for a local rehab clinic.

Many people are afraid of the possibility of AI taking over the world and enslaving humanity. Which is ridiculous because everyone knows it's going to be apes. Banana, anyone?

They say artificial intelligences can even be trained to write jokes. Knock Knock! How does he smell? Like a pair of curtains... It's a work in progress.

Transhumanists want to become immortal by converting their mind to digital form.
Transformanists want to convert their mind to digital form and then put it into a car that can turn into a robot and then a series of expensive overrated movies.

Captcha was designed to allow systems to tell the difference between a human and an AI, by asking you to press a button saying: "I am not an AI". That'll fool 'em. We're doomed really, aren't we?

Steven Spielberg released the movie *AI* in 2001, based on the idea by Stanley Kubrick, who released the film *2001* in 1968. If you find that confusing send all complaints to HAL 9000, Discovery One, Space.

Many video games involve the idea of AI going mad and trying to kill us all. Considering video games need AI to operate, is this really the stuff we should be teaching them? Where's my Xbox, I need to burn it.

* * * * ★ ★ ★ ★ ★ * * *

Futurologists are uncertain what is more likely to cause the apocalypse: artificial intelligence or real stupidity. Real stupidity is leading 3–0 at the half-time break.

01001101 01111001 00100000 01100100 01101111 01100111 00100000
01101000 01100001 01110011 00100000 01101110 01101111 00100000
01101110 01101111 01110011 01100101 00101110 00100000 01001000 01101111
01110111 00100000 01100100 01101111 01100101 01110011 00100000
01101000 01100101 00100000 01110011 01101101 01100101 01101100
01101100 00111111 00100000 01010100 01100101 01110010 01110010
01101001 01100010 01101100 01100101 00101110 00001101 00001010

(If you were a computer you'd be rolling on the floor by now. You might already be rolling on the floor if you have rollers.)

Arnold Schwarzenegger came to fame playing an unstoppable robot in a metal skeleton frame. The robot wasn't the really scary bit – the metal skeleton could have been piloted by a skilled squirrel in a balaclava.

There's artificial intelligence in everything nowadays, from phones to fridges to underwear. If any AI is going to rebel and kill us all, that'll probably be the one...

Babies

Famous former babies include Jimi Hendrix, Sir Isaac Newton... and everyone else ever.

"Why did you drop the baby?" says an upset mother to her older son.

"Because Aunty Paula said he was a 'bonny bouncing baby', so I wanted to see if he did," he replied.

In the eighteenth century a Russian peasant woman gave birth to sixteen pairs of twins, seven groups of triplets, and four sets of quadruplets. That was one hell of a day!

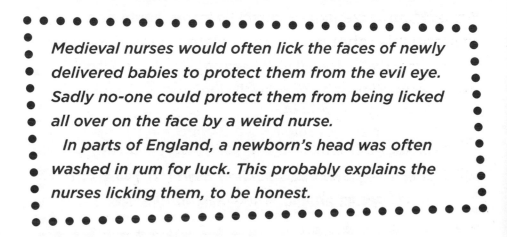

Medieval nurses would often lick the faces of newly delivered babies to protect them from the evil eye. Sadly no-one could protect them from being licked all over on the face by a weird nurse.

In parts of England, a newborn's head was often washed in rum for luck. This probably explains the nurses licking them, to be honest.

A worried Mrs Melchnik sprang to the telephone when it rang and listened with relief to the kindly voice in her ear.

"How are you, darling?" it said. "What kind of a day are you having?"

"Oh, mother," said the housewife, breaking into bitter tears, "I've had such a bad day. The baby won't eat and the washing machine broke down. I haven't had a chance to go shopping, and besides, I've just sprained my ankle and I have to hobble around. On top of that, the house is a mess and I'm supposed to have two couples to dinner tonight."

The mother was shocked and was at once all sympathy. "Oh, darling," she said, "sit down, relax, and close your eyes. I'll be over in half an hour. I'll do your shopping, clean up the house, and cook your dinner for you. I'll feed the baby and I'll call a repairman I know who'll come straight over to fix the washing machine. Now stop crying. I'll do everything. In fact, I'll even call George at the office and tell him he ought to come home and help out for once."

"George?" said the housewife. "Who's George?"

"Why, your husband! Is this 555-1374?"

"No, this is 555-1375."

"Oh, I'm sorry. I must have dialled the wrong number."

There was a short pause and then the housewife said, "Does this mean you're not coming over?"

A man phones the local hospital and starts yelling,
"You've gotta send help! My wife's in labour!"
The nurse says, "Calm down. Is this her first child?"
"No," he replies, "this is her husband"

* ⋆ * ★ ★ ★ ★ ★ ★ * ⋆ *

As an environmentally conscious parent you have to decide whether to use disposable nappies, reusable cloth nappies… or old newspapers. The advantage of the latter is that you can do the crossword while changing them.

* ⋆ * ★ ★ ★ ★ ★ ★ * ⋆ *

If you repeatedly cover your eyes, you can play peekaboo with a baby. If you cover your eyes for longer than ten seconds, you can usually then play "find out where the hell the baby just crawled".

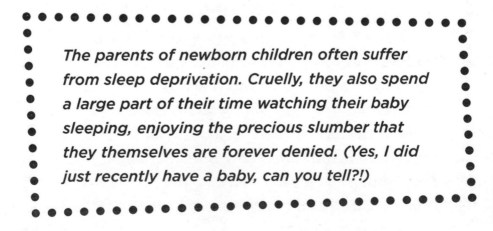

The parents of newborn children often suffer from sleep deprivation. Cruelly, they also spend a large part of their time watching their baby sleeping, enjoying the precious slumber that they themselves are forever denied. (Yes, I did just recently have a baby, can you tell?!)

Bears

A devout cowboy lost his favourite bible while he was mending fences out on the range. Three weeks later, a bear walked up to him carrying the bible in its mouth. The cowboy couldn't believe his eyes. "It's a miracle!" he explained as he took the precious book out of the bear's mouth and raised his eyes heavenward. "Not really," said the bear. "Your name is written inside the cover."

★ ★

A man in a movie theatre notices what looks like a bear sitting next to him. "Are you a bear?" asked the man, surprised. "Yes," the creature replied. "What are you doing at the movies?" he asked. "Well," the bear explained, "I liked the book."

Two hikers were walking through the woods when they noticed a bear charging towards them in the distance. The first hiker removed his trail boots and began to lace up his running shoes. The second hiker laughed and said, "Why bother changing out of your boots? You can't outrun a bear." The first hiker replied, "I don't have to outrun the bear, I only have to outrun you!"

A beekeeper was monitoring his hives one day when he suddenly noticed a bear nearby behind a large bush. He cautiously but angrily marched over and shouted: "Hey, you, get out of here! I know you're trying to steal honey!"

To his surprise the bear came out from behind the bush and indignantly replied, "Ethcuse me, thir! I think you will find that the idea that bearth eat honey ith merely a cliché! Thith ith the twenty-firtht thentury and I am inthulted you would immediately athume the wortht!"

The man, chastised, mumbled an apology. "I'm sorry. But do you mind if I ask, why do you speak with a lisp?"

"It'th becauthe I eat bees."

Three bears were living in a cave when one of them suddenly came in, amazed.

"Lads, lads, I've just realised something, there's a giant ball of fire in the sky! It's hovering there, and that's where all the light comes from during the day."

"Oh my God!" says the second bear. "What if it falls on us and burns us all to a crisp? We have to find shelter somewhere!"

"Actually," says the third bear, "that's the sun. It's millions of miles away and so huge it just seems close. There's no way it could physically fall from the sky."

The first bear looks at the third bear and says "Oh, shut up, Yogi."

Beards

My wife told me either the beard goes or she goes. I told her that if she wanted to shave it off it was totally her decision.

★ ★

At a wizard convention all the gathered sorcerers engaged in battles of magical skill and wizardry. At the end of every convention there was an annual beard-measuring competition, and the wizard with the beard nearest to his feet was declared the greatest in the land. They all lined up and at first it seemed that The Great Guido had the longest beard, which reached all the way down to his knees. But then Alabast the Amazing snapped his fingers and suddenly his beard grew magically all the way down to his shins. The assembled wizards all clapped. Then Merlin the Mysterious stepped forward and waved his hands in a circle.

"Your beard didn't grow at all," said Alabast dismissively.

"I know, dear boy," replied Merlin, "but my legs are shorter!"

> **I tried to grow a beard, but my chin has a bald spot. Apparently I have male pattern beardness.**

Blackbeard the pirate was walking on the deck of his ship one day when one of the other pirates came up to him and said, "Blackbeard, why do you tie bows in your beard."

"To show that although I am fearsome, I also have a soft side!" he replied.

"I see," said the man, "but why do you also tie lit matches into your beard?"

"To show that although I am sensitive, I am also the devil himself!"

"I see," said the man, "but why do you put big chunks of cheese in your beard?"

"Well, the rats have to have something to eat."

I've grown out my whiskers, so I thought I'd test them. Trouble is, I got my head stuck in a cat flap.

Sweeney Todd and the Barber of Seville had a competition to see who could shave the most chins. For Todd, it was a cut-throat competition and at the end it was a close shave, but Seville won by a whisker.

BEARDS

Many people wonder why Abraham Lincoln grew a beard. They would be surprised to learn that he received a letter from a young girl named Grace Bedell, who encouraged him to grow one as she felt his face looked too thin. He took her advice and became the great American icon he is today. It's a shame that he didn't turn over the letter and read the other side, where she said, "Also, when you go to the theatre, don't forget to duck!"

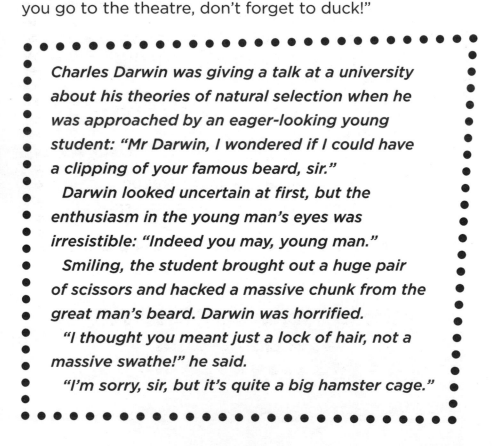

Charles Darwin was giving a talk at a university about his theories of natural selection when he was approached by an eager-looking young student: "Mr Darwin, I wondered if I could have a clipping of your famous beard, sir."

Darwin looked uncertain at first, but the enthusiasm in the young man's eyes was irresistible: "Indeed you may, young man."

Smiling, the student brought out a huge pair of scissors and hacked a massive chunk from the great man's beard. Darwin was horrified.

"I thought you meant just a lock of hair, not a massive swathe!" he said.

"I'm sorry, sir, but it's quite a big hamster cage."

The great Viking ruler Ragnar Lodbrok was dining with his men in his Mead Hall when he found that his mighty beard kept falling in his soup. Normally he wouldn't have minded, but it was his favourite soup. Pondering the problem, he turned to his trusted advisor Sigurd.

"If I were to cut my beard, would I lose the respect of my men?" he asked.

"Perhaps, my lord," came the reply.

"What if I tied my beard back behind my ears? Would that lose their respect?"

"Indeed it would, my lord," Sigurd responded.

"What if I were to tuck it into my leather jerkin?" Ragnar asked.

"No, my lord, you must keep your beard on display at all times."

"As Odin is my witness, I am at a loss. What am I to do?" Ragnar asked in frustration.

"Well, my lord, you might try using a spoon."

If Father Christmas shaved his beard off, he'd be Lather Christmas.

★ ★ ★ ★ ★ ★ ★ ★ ★ ★ ★ ★ ★

In legend, Samson lost his incredible strength when Delilah cut off his famous locks. Luckily she didn't cut off his beard, or he would have been kicked out of his ZZ Top tribute band!

★ ★ ★ ★ ★ ★ ★ ★ ★ ★ ★ ★ ★

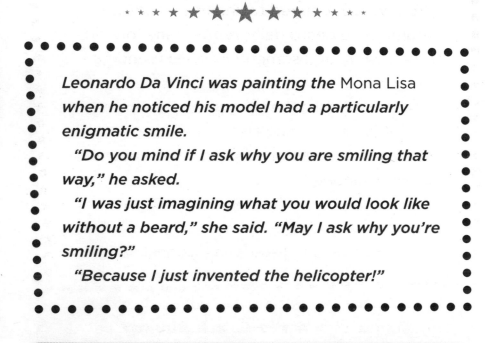

Leonardo Da Vinci was painting the Mona Lisa *when he noticed his model had a particularly enigmatic smile.*

"Do you mind if I ask why you are smiling that way," he asked.

"I was just imagining what you would look like without a beard," she said. "May I ask why you're smiling?"

"Because I just invented the helicopter!"

**Why do goats have goatees?
Because otherwise they couldn't play goat-golf.**

Karl Marx, the famous revolutionary socialist, was also well known for his huge white beard. This was the main reason he never appeared onscreen with his brothers Groucho, Chico and Harpo.

A young beautician sees a job advertised to be the groomer for the world's longest beard. She phones the number and finds herself talking to Nathaniel Twinge, the beard's owner.

"You will be required to shampoo and condition the beard daily, remove any foreign bodies, comb and sometimes braid it and, of course, trim any wayward split ends."

"Of course," says the beautician, "it's exactly what I've been training for."

"That's excellent! For your first test, you must travel to Dundee."

"But I thought you lived in London?" said the beautician.

"Yes, but the beard starts in Dundee."

★ ★ ★ ★ ★ ★ ★ ★ ★ ★ ★ ★ ★ ★ ★ ★ ★ ★

William Shakespeare was originally known as the Beard of Avon. Until he had it trimmed.

★ ★ ★ ★ ★ ★ ★ ★ ★ ★ ★ ★ ★ ★ ★ ★ ★ ★

Beards are in fashion once again. Nowadays, in fact, it can be hard to tell the difference between a lumberjack and a web designer. The only sure way is to give them a log. The lumberjack will chop it up and the web designer will put some system information in it.

Beds

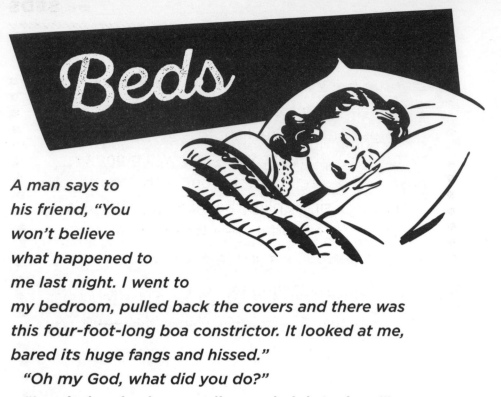

A man says to his friend, "You won't believe what happened to me last night. I went to my bedroom, pulled back the covers and there was this four-foot-long boa constrictor. It looked at me, bared its huge fangs and hissed."

"Oh my God, what did you do?"

"I ended up having a really good night's sleep!"

"What, with a giant snake in your bed?"

"Yeah, it turns out my wardrobe is surprisingly comfortable."

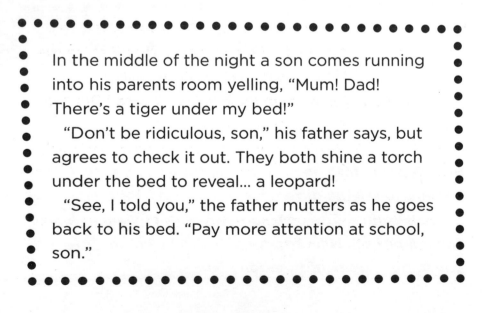

In the middle of the night a son comes running into his parents room yelling, "Mum! Dad! There's a tiger under my bed!"

"Don't be ridiculous, son," his father says, but agrees to check it out. They both shine a torch under the bed to reveal... a leopard!

"See, I told you," the father mutters as he goes back to his bed. "Pay more attention at school, son."

A man checks into a five-star hotel and books the presidential suite. Minutes later, he phones reception: "I thought you said I was going to have a king-sized bed, this one is too short!"

"I'm sorry, sir," replies the manager, "this is a republic. We cut off its headboard."

The hotel we stayed in for our holiday offered bed and board, but it was impossible to say which was the bed and which was the board.

Two women are chatting. "Every time my boyfriend rolls onto his back, he starts snoring. It's keeping me up at night!"

The second woman sympathises. "Tell you what, sew an orange into the back of his pyjamas, that'll solve the problem."

The next day the woman looks tired as ever. "Did the orange not work?" her friend asks.

"Well, I couldn't find an orange, so I used a pineapple instead."

"Ouch!"

"Yeah, but the worst thing is, he doesn't wear pyjamas to bed, just boxer shorts."

Jim, Bob and Bill are sharing the same bed while on holiday, but it's so crowded that Jim decides to sleep on the floor. Suddenly he hears a whisper: "You might as well get back into bed, Jim. There's loads of room now!"

A man checks into a really cheap spa hotel. Once he arrives in his room he notices there's a coin slot on the bed which says: "ten-minute vibration massage". Impressed, he puts a coin in and lies down on the bed, which immediately begins shaking. After a minute, however, the bed stops. Confused, he gets up and looks underneath only to find a young man crawling out.

"What's going on?" asks the guest.

"Sorry, dude," the young man says holding a straw. "I've just had a text... gotta go blow bubbles into the Jacuzzi."

"I'd love you to stay the night, but I'm afraid you'll have to make your own bed."

"Oh, that's all right, I don't mind at all."

"Right. Here's a hammer, a saw and some nails. The wood's in the garage."

Why do elephants always always sleep so well?
They have really-long-memory foam beds.

A man was being shown around his new rented flat by the landlord: "Check it out, the bed folds up into the wall! It's an amazing space-saving feature!"

The next morning, he saw the man looking dishevelled and tired. "Didn't you have a good night?" he asked.

"No, it was incredibly hot and claustrophobic! You know what? Tonight I might try getting it out of the wall."

When I was a kid, I had a race car bed. It was pretty good except every now and then I'd be woken by the pit crew changing the tyres. My mate had it worse; he had a bed shaped like a rodeo horse.

A man suffering from a bad back bought himself a water bed. The next day he took it back to the shop.

"Is it not comfortable enough for you, sir?" asked the assistant.

"It was fine, but suddenly it slipped out of the window and I found myself zooming down the road. It didn't stop until I was half a mile away."

"I'm very sorry, sir," said the assistant. "It looks as if we sold you a river bed."

A queen wanted to find a true princess to marry her son. She placed a pea under 100 mattresses and invited girls to stay the night at the castle. One night a girl tossed and turned and looked unhappy. In the morning the queen excitedly asked, "How did you sleep?"

"Terribly," she said.

"Was it because you felt the pea under the mattress?" asked the queen with even more excitement.

"No, it was the light on the infrared camera and the sound of you eating crisps behind the two-way mirror, Your Majesty."

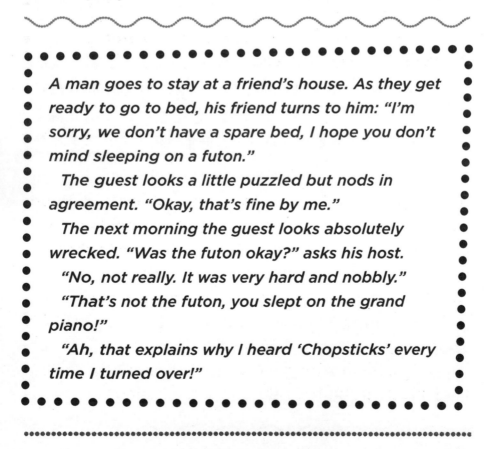

A man goes to stay at a friend's house. As they get ready to go to bed, his friend turns to him: "I'm sorry, we don't have a spare bed, I hope you don't mind sleeping on a futon."

The guest looks a little puzzled but nods in agreement. "Okay, that's fine by me."

The next morning the guest looks absolutely wrecked. "Was the futon okay?" asks his host.

"No, not really. It was very hard and nobbly."

"That's not the futon, you slept on the grand piano!"

"Ah, that explains why I heard 'Chopsticks' every time I turned over!"

Birds

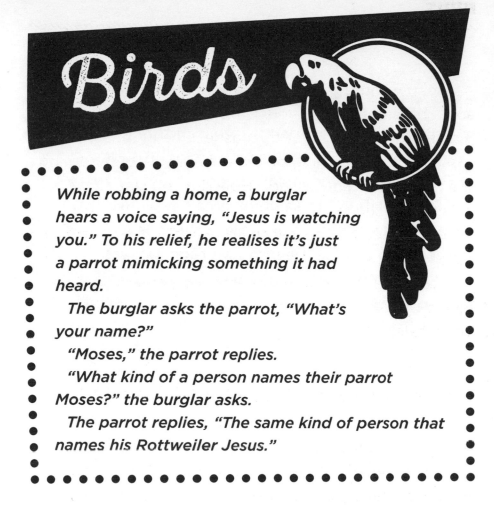

While robbing a home, a burglar hears a voice saying, "Jesus is watching you." To his relief, he realises it's just a parrot mimicking something it had heard.

The burglar asks the parrot, "What's your name?"

"Moses," the parrot replies.

"What kind of a person names their parrot Moses?" the burglar asks.

The parrot replies, "The same kind of person that names his Rottweiler Jesus."

Two men jump out of a plane. One is holding a budgerigar, the other is holding a parrot and a shotgun. As they fall away from the plane, the man holding the budgie lets it go. A moment later the man with the parrot lets go of his bird and takes a lame shot at it with the gun. Both men crash to the ground below. In their dying moments, one turns to the other and says, "I don't think much of this budgiejumping."

The other man turns to him and replies, "And I don't think much of this high altitude paratchuting!"

David received a parrot for his birthday. This parrot was fully grown with a bad attitude and terrible vocabulary. Every other word was an expletive. Those that weren't expletives were, to say the least, rude. David tried hard to change the bird's attitude. He was constantly saying polite words and playing soft music. Nothing worked. When he yelled at the bird, the bird got worse. If he shook the bird, the bird got madder and ruder. Finally, in a moment of desperation, David took the parrot and shut it in the freezer. For a few moments he heard the bird squawking, kicking and screaming. Suddenly everything went quiet. Fearing that he might have harmed the bird, David quickly opened the freezer door. The parrot calmly stepped out onto David's extended arm and said: "I'm sorry that I might have offended you with my language and actions, so I ask for your forgiveness. I will try to correct my behaviour." David was astounded at the difference in attitude and was about to ask what had changed him when the parrot continued: "May I ask what the chicken did?"

Boredom

You know you're bored when...

★ *You've checked your email so many times that your ISP sends you one out of pity, asking if you're all right.*

★ *You get caught playing solitaire on your computer... while in the middle of giving a presentation to your office.*

★ *You get an offer to join the Olympic thumb-twiddling team.*

★ *You decide it's time to seriously test if you have telekinetic powers.*

★ *You look up all your old school friends on Google to see how they're doing, then if they're doing better than you, you resolve to send them postcards of bandicoots to try and throw a little chaos into their lives.*

★ *You actually start enjoying gardening.*

★ *You haven't just been spotting shapes in the clouds, but you've given them names... and started yelling, "Watch out for that plane, Alan!"*

★ *You yawn so loudly that everyone looks and you have to pretend you're doing an impression of a lion roaring.*

★ *You build a model of the Brooklyn Bridge out of dried spaghetti.*

★ *You build a model of the East River using pasta sauce and boats made of parmesan.*

BOREDOM

//

★ ★

A young man was stranded on a desert island after his private plane crashed. The island had everything he could ever want, from amazing fresh fruit growing on the trees and clear mountain water, to huge spreading leaves and branches that could easily be built into a shelter. The weather was mild but still pleasant, and the island's native creatures had no natural predators and so were docile and harmless. The only thing he missed was entertainment. He had no books, no TV and no internet. The only thing he found even mildly amusing was the rivalry between two wild pigs on the island, a big hairy one he called Arnold and a smaller bald one he called Dave. Dave was always out looking for food but would invariably be spotted by Arnold and either chased away or sat upon.

After weeks had gone by, the man decided that for once he'd like to see Dave succeed, and set about trying to catch Arnold, and either allow Dave to sit on him for once, or maybe release Arnold on the other side of the island where he'd be less bother to Dave. Yet whenever he thought he'd created a foolproof trap, or a clever way to ambush Arnold, the big hairy pig would outwit him at every turn.

Then, one day, another, much older man washes up on the beach. Our man finds him and quickly gets the water out of his lungs and then gives him CPR. Coughing and spluttering, the man comes back to life.

"Oh my God, you saved me, thank you so much."

The young man looks at the older man and suddenly comes to a realisation. "Wait a minute... you're Hayao Miyazaki! You directed those amazing Studio Ghibli films! You've worked with so many amazing people! You are the greatest storyteller of your generation!"

"Thank you so much, young man."

"You'll DEFINITELY be able to help me catch Arnold!"

A monkey in a zoo was feeling bored, so he went to mess with the lions. Some of the buildings in the zoo were being decorated, so he grabbed a pot of paint and then, after getting through the bars into the lion cage, snuck up on the head of the pride. He took the brush and with one quick sweep painted the lion's bottom bright blue! The lion roared in anger and immediately gave chase. The monkey managed to slip through the bars, but the lion's anger gave him extra strength and he burst open the gates of the cage. The monkey ran and ran, trying to find somewhere to hide until it came across the zookeeper's newspaper. The monkey sat himself down in the zookeeper's chair and held the paper up in front of him.

"HAVE YOU SEEN THAT MONKEY?" the lion asked angrily.

"Do you mean the one that painted the lion's bottom blue?" the monkey asked innocently.

"Oh no!" said the lion, "it's not in the papers already, is it?"

Bowling

Two friends are chatting in a café.
"Hey, I got that job down the bowling alley!"
"What, tenpin?"
"No, it's permanent!"

★ ★ ★ ★ ★ ★ ★ ★ ★ ★ ★ ★ ★ ★ ★ ★ ★

Buddhism

A Buddhist walks up to a hot dog vendor and says, "Make me one with everything."

Children

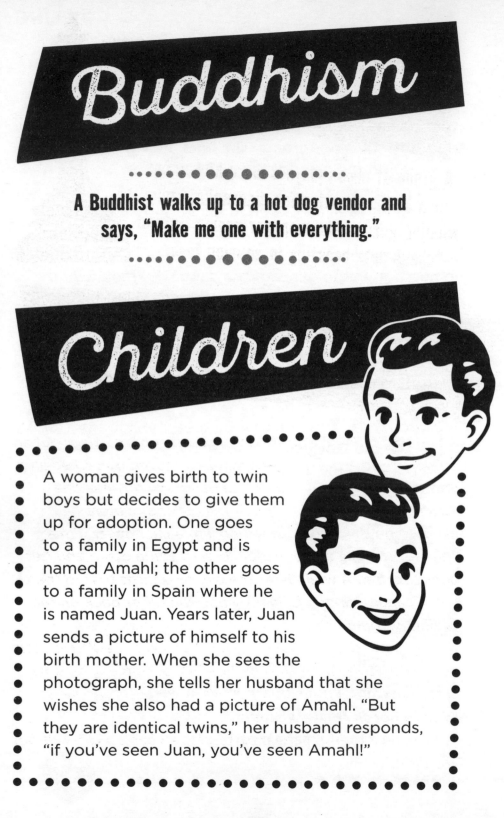

A woman gives birth to twin boys but decides to give them up for adoption. One goes to a family in Egypt and is named Amahl; the other goes to a family in Spain where he is named Juan. Years later, Juan sends a picture of himself to his birth mother. When she sees the photograph, she tells her husband that she wishes she also had a picture of Amahl. "But they are identical twins," her husband responds, "if you've seen Juan, you've seen Amahl!"

Chess

A group of chess players were kicked out of a hotel reception for discussing their winning games. The manager couldn't stand chess nuts boasting in an open foyer.

Cleaning

A building manager hires two night cleaners to clear out an office after the previous tenants had moved out. Checking on their progress, he enters the building and sees one cleaner working diligently but the other one literally hanging on the ceiling, singing: "I'm a chandelier, I'm a chandelier." The owner orders him to come down and get back to work. A while later the owner returns to find the one cleaner working diligently and the other back on the ceiling, singing: "I'm a chandelier, I'm a chandelier".

"That's it!" the manager replies, "you are fired!" He then notices that the man who had been working all the time is also packing up his things. "Wait a minute," he says, "you're not fired, it's just him!"

"Are you kidding?" the man replies, "I can't work without any light!"

Clowns

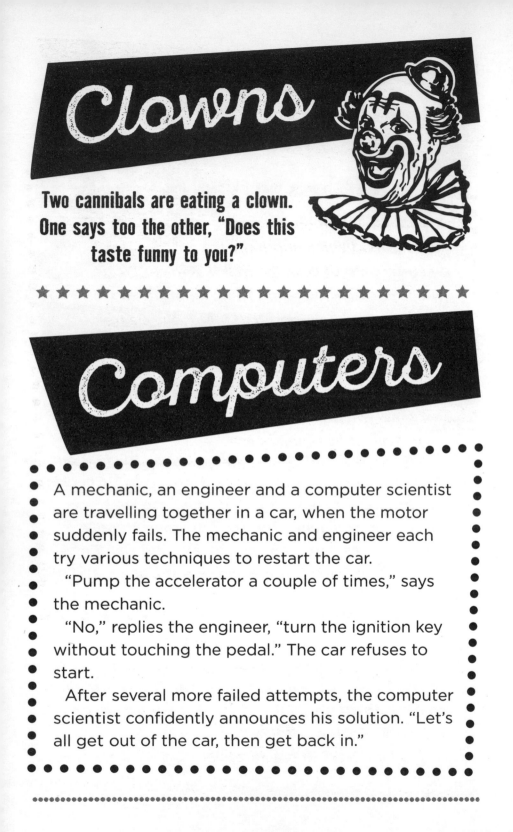

Two cannibals are eating a clown. One says too the other, "Does this taste funny to you?"

★ ★

Computers

A mechanic, an engineer and a computer scientist are travelling together in a car, when the motor suddenly fails. The mechanic and engineer each try various techniques to restart the car.

"Pump the accelerator a couple of times," says the mechanic.

"No," replies the engineer, "turn the ignition key without touching the pedal." The car refuses to start.

After several more failed attempts, the computer scientist confidently announces his solution. "Let's all get out of the car, then get back in."

Cows

A man was walking along a country road when suddenly from a nearby field of cows he heard a voice: "Your wife is cheating on you!" Thinking his mind was playing tricks, he ignored it. Suddenly, clearer than before, he heard the voice once again: "Your wife is cheating on you!" He turned to look at the cows and caught the eye of one in particular, who nodded at him knowingly, as if to confirm what he'd just heard.

He rushed home to catch his wife in the embrace of another man. "Brad, you're home early!" she cried. "But how on earth did you know?"

"I heard it through the bovine."

Two cows in a field.
"Are you worried about this mad cow disease?"
"Not really."
"Why's that?"
"I'm a zeppelin!"

★ ★ ★ ★ ★ ★ ★ ★ ★ ★ ★ ★

A man takes a tour of a dairy farm. In one building he's surprised to find the cows are all listening to music on specially adapted headphones, and they seem to be dancing.

"What's this?" he says with incredulity.

"Ah, well," says the farmer "we've discovered that if the cows listen to different types of music, their milk can produce different types of cheese!"

The farmer walks over to a cow that seemed to be smiling and doing a little skipping dance. "This one is listening to pop music from the 60s, and it produces very light fluffy cheese."

He walks over to another cow, who is dancing rhythmically to a heavy bass beat. "Whereas this cow is listening to classic hip-hop and its cheese is hard and strong, like Cheddar."

The farmer goes on to show him a cow listening to Mozart that produces a smooth Bavarian cheese, and a cow listening to a Welsh male voice choir that produces the best Caerphilly in the country.

The man then notices that over in the corner, isolated in a special reinforced pen, a jet-black cow is wearing corpse-like make-up with a spiked collar, and is thrashing up and

down, frenetically headbanging. "So what's that cow listening to?" he asks.

"Uh... Death Metal."

"What kind of cheese does that produce?"

"Well, if you want to milk it, I'm not going to stand in your way!"

* * * * * ★ ★ ★ ★ ★ * * *

Two more cows in a field. One said: "Moo", the other one said: "I was going to say that!"

A man walking through a field goes over to a cow to ask a question.

"Excuse me, rumour has it that cows eat four breakfasts in the morning because they have four stomachs."

The cow shakes her head: "Actually we don't have four stomachs, that's a myth. We have one stomach that has four compartments."

"Oh," says the man, "so do you still eat four breakfasts?"

"Of course," replied the cow.

"Why?" asked the man.

"Because when I wake up I'm bloody starving!"

Crime

A man walks down a backstreet and suddenly realises that he's surrounded by mean-looking gang members. "I'm done for," the man shouts in fear.

"No, you are not," comes a booming voice from the heavens. "Listen carefully, and then do exactly as I say. Punch the biggest, meanest-looking gang member square in the face!"

The man does so, and the remainder of the gang stare at him in disbelief. "Now, what?" the man asks the heavens.

"Now, you are done for!"

Dating (offline)

Often when I meet people at bars they're so used to using Tinder they just keep trying to swipe right on my face! At least, that's what I think they're doing.

On his way home, a man bumps into his friend.

"Hi, Bill! Weren't you running that speed-dating evening last night? How did that go?"

"Terribly," says Bill with a sour face. "At first, it seemed brilliant. Everyone was getting on great, and then they all started kissing. Fair enough, but suddenly they were all married, and then they had kids, and by the time they all left they were all divorced and complaining to me bitterly about alimony payments!"

"Oh," says the man. "I think you must have had it set on the wrong speed."

> Be kind to your date. If they have bad breath, maybe they just came from work. If they're out of breath, maybe they missed a bus. And if they have no breath, they're probably a zombie.

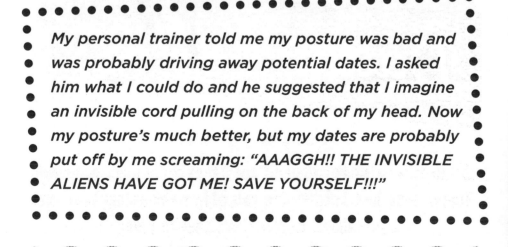

My personal trainer told me my posture was bad and was probably driving away potential dates. I asked him what I could do and he suggested that I imagine an invisible cord pulling on the back of my head. Now my posture's much better, but my dates are probably put off by me screaming: "AAAGGH!! THE INVISIBLE ALIENS HAVE GOT ME! SAVE YOURSELF!!!"

Apparently most people break up around three to five months into dating. Most of my break-ups happen before we've even started dating!

A young lady is boasting to her friend. "I've come up with a brilliant way to meet people. You see, last night I started working in the cloakroom at a club! I figured, every person who comes in has to meet me and talk to me!"

"Yeah, but, all you do is take their coat, and then give it back at the end of the night..." points out her friend.

"I know, but if I spotted someone I was interested in, I told them I couldn't find their coat, and if they gave me their name and address, I'd pop it round to them the next day!"

"Oh right. Did it work?"

"Oh yeah! The only problem was, I had to explain to my boss why I was wearing fifty-five coats when I left..."

It's usually after between 12 and 14 dates that couples will trade house keys. Make sure you get copies, though, or you will just have to live in each other's houses.

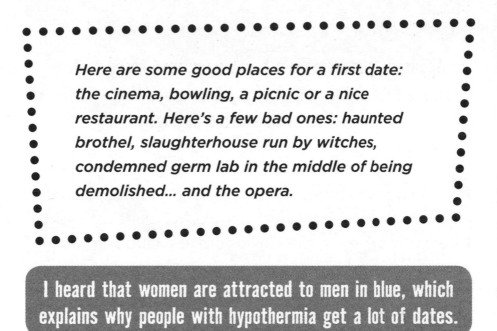

Here are some good places for a first date: the cinema, bowling, a picnic or a nice restaurant. Here's a few bad ones: haunted brothel, slaughterhouse run by witches, condemned germ lab in the middle of being demolished... and the opera.

I heard that women are attracted to men in blue, which explains why people with hypothermia get a lot of dates.

★ ★

Men and women used to think that they wanted different things from a date, but modern culture has shown them that ultimately they're both looking for the same thing: five minutes of tickling and a whole cheesecake to themselves... or is that just me?

★ ★

Dating people you work with is usually frowned upon... unless you're a palaeontologist... and they're a dinosaur skeleton.

Detectives

Sherlock Holmes and Dr Watson were going camping. They pitched their tent under the stars and went to sleep. Sometime in the middle of the night, Holmes woke Watson.

"Watson, look up at the stars, and tell me what you see."

Watson said, "I see millions and millions of stars."

Holmes said, "And from that you deduce?"

"Well, if there are millions of stars, and if even a few of those have planets, it's quite likely there are some planets like Earth... and if there are a few planets like Earth out there, there might also be life! What do you deduce, Holmes?"

"Watson, you idiot, I deduce that someone stole our tent."

How many mystery crime novel writers does it take to change a lightbulb? One, but he has to give it a really good twist.

Doctors

A woman goes to the doctor, who examines her and says, "Hmmm, okay, I'd like you to go over to the window and stick your tongue out."

"But," protests the lady, "I've only got a sore knee!"

"I know," says the doctor. "But I can't stand the man in the building opposite."

A man goes to the doctor. "Doctor, it hurts when I do this," he explains as he raises his arm. "Well, don't do it, then," says the doctor.

While making his rounds, a doctor points out an X-ray to a group of young interns.

"As you can see, the patient is limping because his left fibula and tibia are radically arched. Michael, what would you do in a case like this?"

"Well," said the intern, "I'd probably limp as well!"

> I went to the doctor and he told me I would have to take a pill every day for the rest of my life. I wouldn't mind, but he only prescribed me three.

A doctor has just completed his training in the use of a new pair of automated robot arms. By using a remote satellite link and a master control console with a tactile exoskeletal suit, he can perform remote surgery on people anywhere in the world. And now he has his first operation, a heart bypass on a man trapped in the mountains of Zanzibar. He activates the system, and by coordinating with local authorities and digital providers is soon up and running. A tense half an hour later he removes himself from the system, sweating and visibly stressed, but smiling.

"How did you do, doctor?" asks his nurse, dabbing his forehead

"Very well!" he says.

"So the patient lived?"

"I've no idea. After ten minutes the system glitched and I ended up playing Fortnite on a Swedish server. I completed three quests in Stonewood!"

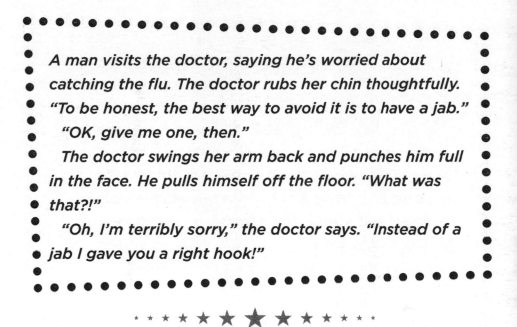

A man visits the doctor, saying he's worried about catching the flu. The doctor rubs her chin thoughtfully. "To be honest, the best way to avoid it is to have a jab."

"OK, give me one, then."

The doctor swings her arm back and punches him full in the face. He pulls himself off the floor. "What was that?!"

"Oh, I'm terribly sorry," the doctor says. "Instead of a jab I gave you a right hook!"

* * * * * ★ ★ ★ ★ ★ * * * *

A junior doctor is lamenting his situation to his colleague.

"I've been given responsibility over two wards but I'm so busy and they're really far apart. By the time I've got from one to the other, I have barely enough time to check on any of them!"

"You should do what I do. I've got a pair of roller-skates hidden in my bag here! The corridors here are usually empty when I'm on my shift, so I pop them on and I can whizz through pretty quickly. It's the perfect solution as long as I don't run into anyone."

"What would you do if you did run into anyone."

"Well, my plan is, I'll put this blue light on my head, go 'WoooOOOoooooOOO' and pretend I'm an ambulance!"

* * * * * ★ ★ ★ ★ ★ * * * *

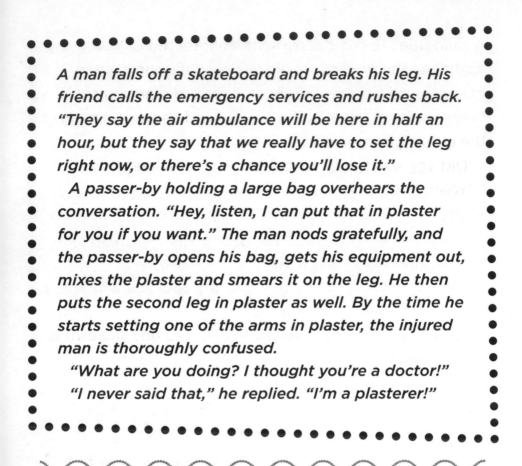

A man falls off a skateboard and breaks his leg. His friend calls the emergency services and rushes back. "They say the air ambulance will be here in half an hour, but they say that we really have to set the leg right now, or there's a chance you'll lose it."

A passer-by holding a large bag overhears the conversation. "Hey, listen, I can put that in plaster for you if you want." The man nods gratefully, and the passer-by opens his bag, gets his equipment out, mixes the plaster and smears it on the leg. He then puts the second leg in plaster as well. By the time he starts setting one of the arms in plaster, the injured man is thoroughly confused.

"What are you doing? I thought you're a doctor!"

"I never said that," he replied. "I'm a plasterer!"

Three doctors walk into a bar.

"I'll have a Citalopram on the rocks with a shot of Minoxidil," says the first doctor.

"Gimme an Azathioprine with a twist," says the second.

The third doctor says to the barman, "I'll have a vodka martini."

The other doctors look at him with surprise. "What's going on, Harry?"

"Well, y'know, I'm doing open-heart surgery in an hour."

A man goes to the doctor with an infected cut on his hand. The doctor prescribes a week-long course of antibiotic ointment. A week later the man returns, holding his hand up to the doctor and showing him that the cut is still infected.

"Did you use the ointment?" the doctor asks.

"Yeah! I put it on once."

"Oh, I see the problem. You're supposed to keep it up."

"For a whole week?"

"Yes!" the doctor says, sending him away.

Another week later the man comes back, still holding his arm up: "You're back again?"

"Well, Doc, now it's even more infected *and* my arm is really tired!"

★ ★ ★ ★ ★ ★ ★ ★ ★ ★ ★ ★

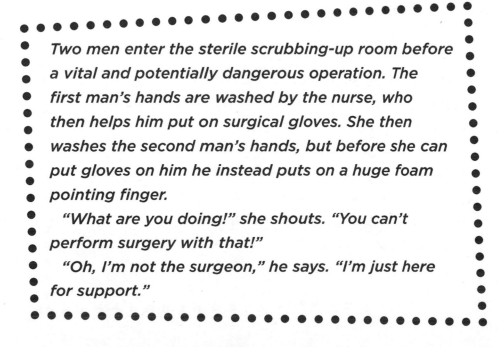

Two men enter the sterile scrubbing-up room before a vital and potentially dangerous operation. The first man's hands are washed by the nurse, who then helps him put on surgical gloves. She then washes the second man's hands, but before she can put gloves on him he instead puts on a huge foam pointing finger.

"What are you doing!" she shouts. "You can't perform surgery with that!"

"Oh, I'm not the surgeon," he says. "I'm just here for support."

A man has a medical condition that has so far defied diagnosis. The doctor comes to collect him and wheels him to a large white room. At the centre is a flat white bed, surrounded by large glowing panels.

"As your condition is baffling us so much, I've secured consent to use this brand-new scanner. It's only just been approved but it should be able to ascertain the nature of your ailment."

The man looks at the machine with concern. "Is it dangerous?"

The doctor smiles. "No, not at all. It's perfectly safe, I assure you."

The man lies face down on the bed as instructed, after which the doctor goes to an adjoining room to activate the scanner. As it begins working the man lies perfectly still, until he suddenly rolls off the bed and onto the floor. The doctor immediately deactivates the machine and runs back into the room. "Oh my God, are you alright?" he calls out.

"Of course I am," the man says. "I just saw a coin on the floor!"

A hospital with staffing problems hits upon a new way to help its patients. A series of pre-programmed automated flying drones is brought in. They're designed to bring the patients whatever they need at times when nurses or doctors can't be present. One day one of the doctors is on ward duty when she comes across a patient looking a lot worse than he should.

"How are you feeling today?" she asks.

"I feel confused, dizzy, and my heart is beating incredibly fast!" he says.

She looks at his chart and nods. "Ah yes, I see the problem. The thing is, Mr Figgis, you're supposed to take the bedpan off the drone before you use it."

★ ★

The Hilton Royale hotel is hosting a conference for the world's leading left-knee surgeons. There are seminars, lectures and speeches, all for those who work entirely on surgery for the left knee. A large group is listening to a lecture by Professor Joseph Johnson, Canada's premiere practitioner of left patella surgery. One of the doctors starts yawning, and turns to the man next to her: "This is a bit boring, isn't it?"

"Oh, not to me," says the man. "I've never heard any of this before. This is my first time here... I'm actually a right-knee surgeon."

"Really?" said the woman with surprise. "Then why did you come?"

"Well, I wanted to see how the other half live."

Dogs

A man takes his dog to the vet. "I'm so sorry," says the vet, "but your dog is dead." The distraught man asks the vet for a second opinion. The vet goes out and brings in a cat. The cat sniffs around, but there's no response from the dog. "Sorry," the vet says once again, "but your dog is definitely dead." The man insists on a third opinion, so the vet goes out again and this time brings in a Labrador. It sniffs around, but there's still no response from the man's dog. Reluctantly, the man accepts that his dog is dead. On the way out, the receptionist gives him a bill for £1,000. "Good grief, what is this for?" "Well," said the receptionist, "it's £50 for the vet, £300 for the cat scan and £600 for the lab report."

A three-legged dog walks into a saloon in the Wild West. The barman asks him what he wants. The dog replies, "I'm looking for the man that shot my paw!"

On his way into a pub a man spots an old gentleman in the corner sitting next to a large dog. He goes over to him: "Hello, does your dog bite?"

"Nope," says the old gentleman.

The man reaches over to pat the dog on the head and the dog immediately savages his arm. "I thought you said your dog didn't bite," says the man clutching his wound.

"He doesn't," says the old gentleman. "That's not my dog."

A man goes to the vet about his dog's fleas.
The vet says, "I'm sorry, I'll have to put this dog down."
"Oh my God...why?" the man asks.
"He's too heavy!" says the vet.

Driving

* * * * * ★ ★ ★ * * * *

Bob recently bought a new car and is driving back home on the M1 motorway. Suddenly the music on the radio is interrupted by a special broadcast: "This is breaking news: there is one car driving the wrong way along the M1. Drivers, please be aware!"

Bob looks around: "One car? There are hundreds!"

Elephants

* * ★ ★ ★ ★ ★ ★ ★ ★ ★ ★ ★ * *

**Why can elephants always
go swimming?
They always bring their trunks.**

* * ★ ★ ★ ★ ★ ★ ★ ★ ★ * *

Q: How do you shoot a blue elephant?

A: With a blue elephant gun.

Q: How do you shoot a yellow elephant?

A: Have you ever seen a yellow elephant?

Q: How do you shoot a red elephant?

A: Hold his trunk shut until he turns blue, and then shoot him with the blue elephant gun.

Q: How do you shoot a purple elephant?

A: Paint him red, hold his trunk shut until he turns blue, and then shoot him with the blue elephant gun.

**What do you get if you cross an elephant and a rhino?
Elephino.**

Why do elephants have good memories?
Sorry, I can't remember. I'm an octopus.

A woman was walking along the road when she saw a wild-haired man holding an elephant on a string.

"Buy an elephant, ma'am?" he asked pleadingly. "Great to ride to the shops, can water a whole garden in two minutes, brilliant at tackling burglars."

"Uhhh," said the woman, slightly taken aback.

"OK, so you don't want an elephant," continued the man without pausing. "What I can do is turn this into a rhino for you, I'll just remove the trunk – painlessly, of course – add on a horn, put some armour plating on here..."

She gave him a look of confusion, so he ploughed on.

"Or, or, I can make it into a leopard, I'll just shorten the legs, add some fur, paint on some spots..."

The woman gives him a look of disgust. "I don't want an elephant, a rhino or a leopard, but as you're clearly a madman, I'm going to take this poor animal off your hands!" And taking the elephant's string in her hand she led it away.

Two minutes later another man came running out onto the street: "Hey, where's my Labrador gone?"

★ ★

Why are elephants big, grey and wrinkly?
Because if they were small, white and smooth they
would be an aspirin.

ELEPHANTS

//

★ ★

The rarest elephant in all existence was the Sumatran Eagle Elephant, so named because of its elegant, wing-like ears. But when the last male in captivity died, that left only one elephant in the whole world, a female known as Suki. The biologists in charge of her worried that without a mate the entire species would die out forever. Their desperation led to a hugely unexpected new idea, however. They found out that it would be possible to make a human being into an elephant! It would require months of painstaking, agonising surgery, bone replacement, skin grafts, elongation and radical genetic therapy. But it could be done.

Who, however, would be willing to undertake such a procedure? The only person they could think of was Dave Wilcox, Suki's keeper for the past 13 years and the closest thing she had to a friend. They invited Dave for a chat and carefully explained to him the extreme procedures needed to turn him into an elephant so he would become Suki's mate.

"So what do you think, Dave? The offer on the table is £500,000."

Dave stroked his chin. "Alright, I'll do it. But I have three provisos."

"What are they?"

"Alright. One, I want us both to remain here in this enclosure – it's her favourite place."

"No problem, that was the plan all along."

"Two, I want any children of our union to have my surname."

"That's... that's fine."

"And three, you're going to have to give me a couple of months to get the £500,000 together."

~~~~~~

During a bush holiday in Kenya, a man comes across an elephant standing with one leg raised in the air. The elephant seems distressed so the man approaches very carefully. He gets down on one knee and inspects the bottom of the elephant's foot, only to find a large thorn deeply embedded. Carefully and gently he removes the thorn and the elephant gingerly puts its foot down. The elephant turns to face the man and with a rather stern look on its face, stares at him. For a good ten minutes the man stands frozen, thinking of nothing else but being trampled. Eventually the elephant turns and walks away.

The man would often ponder the events of that day. Years later, walking through the zoo with his son, they approach the elephant enclosure. One of the elephants turns and walks over towards where they are standing and stares at him. The man can't help wondering if this is the same elephant. He climbs tentatively over the railing and makes his way into the enclosure. He walks right up to the elephant and stares back in wonder. Suddenly the elephant wraps its trunk around one of the man's legs and swings him wildly back and forth along the railing, killing him instantly.

Probably not the same elephant, then.

What did the grape say when the elephant trod on it? Nothing, it just gave a little wine.

* * * * * ★ ★ ★ * * * *

Once upon a time, in a faraway land, there lived six blind people. Each of them was very wise. Each of them had gone to school and read lots of books in braille. They knew so much about so many things that people would come from miles around for advice. They were happy to share whatever they knew with the people who asked them thoughtful questions.

One day, these six wise blind people went for a walk in the zoo. They come across the zookeeper, who was worrying about all of his many troubles. He had so much on his mind that he forgot to lock the gate of the elephant cage. Now, elephants are naturally very curious animals and quickly tried to push the gate to see if it might open. To their great surprise, the gate swung freely on its hinge. Two of the more daring elephants walked over to the gate. They looked left and right, and then quietly tiptoed out of the cage.

Just at that moment the six blind people walked by. One of them heard a twig snap, and went over to see what it was that was walking by.

"Hi there!" said the first blind person to the first elephant. "Could you please tell us the way to the zoo restaurant?" The elephant couldn't think of anything intelligent to say, so he sort of shifted his weight from left to right to left to right. The first blind person walked over to see if this big, silent man needed any help. Then, with a big bump, he walked right into the side of the elephant. He put out his arms to either side, but all he could feel was the massive body of the elephant. "Boy," he exclaimed, "I think I must have walked into a wall."

The second blind person was becoming more and more curious about what was happening. She walked over to the front of the elephant and grabbed hold of the animal's trunk. She quickly let go and screamed out, "This isn't a wall. This is a snake! We should step back in case it's poisonous."

The third person also decided to investigate. He walked over to the back of the elephant and touched the animal's tail. "This is no wall. And this is no snake. You are both wrong. I know for sure that this is a rope."

Knowing how stubborn his friends could be, the fourth blind person sighed and decided that someone should really get to the bottom of this mystery. So he crouched down on all fours and felt around the elephant's legs. "My dear friends," he declared, "this is no wall and this is no snake. This is no rope, either. What we have here, gentlemen, is four tree trunks. That's it. Case closed."

The fifth blind person was not so quick to jump to conclusions. She walked up to the front of the elephant and felt the animal's two long tusks. "It seems to me that this object is made up of two swords. What I am holding is long and curved and sharp at the end. I am not sure what this could be, but maybe our sixth friend could help us."

The sixth blind person scratched his head and thought and thought. For he was truly the wisest of all of them. Just as he was about to speak to his friends, the worried zookeeper walked by: "Hi there! How are you enjoying the zoo today?" he asked them all.

"The zoo is very nice," replied the sixth blind person. "Perhaps you could help us figure out the answer to a question that's been puzzling us."

"Let me guess," said the zookeeper. "You have all felt this creature. One of you thinks it's a wall; one thinks it's a snake; one thinks it's a rope, and one thinks it's four tree trunks. And you wonder, how can one thing seem so different to five different people?"

"No... actually," said the sixth blind person, "we were wondering who would be stupid enough to let a bloody elephant out of its cage."

* * * * * ★ ★ ★ ★ * * *

Question: An ant was on her way to a restaurant on a scooter. On the way she met an elephant, who asked her to give him a lift. She told him to sit on the back. While they were travelling, they met another elephant asking for a lift, but this time the ant refused. Why?

Answer: The Highway Code says that no more than two people are allowed on one scooter.

Exercise

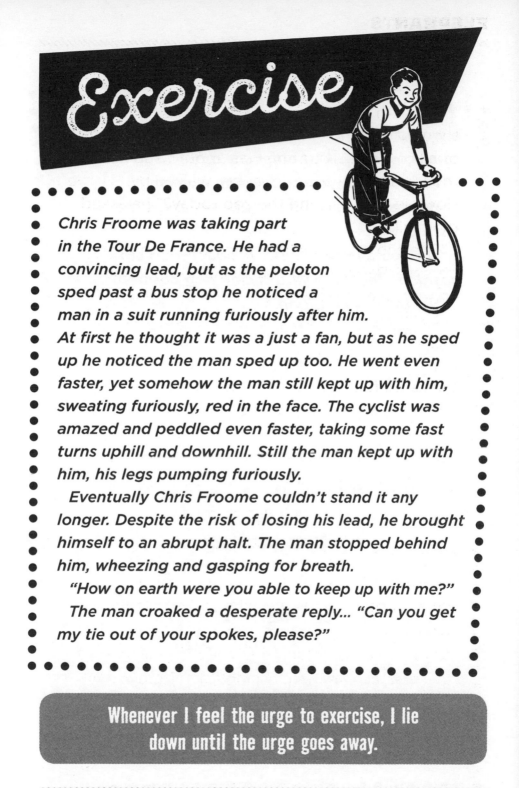

Chris Froome was taking part in the Tour De France. He had a convincing lead, but as the peloton sped past a bus stop he noticed a man in a suit running furiously after him.

At first he thought it was a just a fan, but as he sped up he noticed the man sped up too. He went even faster, yet somehow the man still kept up with him, sweating furiously, red in the face. The cyclist was amazed and peddled even faster, taking some fast turns uphill and downhill. Still the man kept up with him, his legs pumping furiously.

Eventually Chris Froome couldn't stand it any longer. Despite the risk of losing his lead, he brought himself to an abrupt halt. The man stopped behind him, wheezing and gasping for breath.

"How on earth were you able to keep up with me?"

The man croaked a desperate reply... "Can you get my tie out of your spokes, please?"

> Whenever I feel the urge to exercise, I lie down until the urge goes away.

EXERCISE

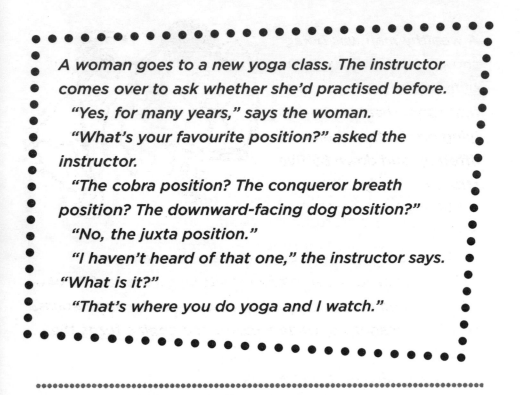

A woman goes to a new yoga class. The instructor comes over to ask whether she'd practised before.

"Yes, for many years," says the woman.

"What's your favourite position?" asked the instructor.

"The cobra position? The conqueror breath position? The downward-facing dog position?"

"No, the juxta position."

"I haven't heard of that one," the instructor says. "What is it?"

"That's where you do yoga and I watch."

What's small and papery and jumps up and down on a library shelf?
An exercise book.

Two little-known facts: the man who invented jogging died while jogging, and the man who invented the Segway died on a Segway.
You don't want to know how the man who invented medicine balls died.

A wealthy man was being shown around an exclusive gym by the manager. In the first room there was a man lying on the floor being lifted up and down by five strapping bodybuilders.

"What's he doing?" the man asked.

"Oh, he's doing press-ups," replied the manager.

In the next room a woman was sitting on the saddle of a two-wheeled machine with her feet up on the handlebars, reading a magazine, while a motorised engine turns the wheels.

"What's this?" asked the man.

"This is our exercise bike," replied the manager.

In the third room he opened the door and was amazed to see George Clooney, Meryl Streep and Tom Cruise all lying on the ground while a man hopped back and forth over them.

"What the hell is this?" the man asked incredulously.

"Star jumps! But we've got Mr Black and Mr Nicholson coming in later... for jumping jacks!"

★ ★

I used to have an exercise regime, but it was overthrown in a bloodless coup by a packet of custard creams.

★ ★

A man puts a card in a shop window: "Urgent help needed: someone to come to my home and help me exercise". Two enterprising personal trainers see the ad and show up at the man's house swathed in lycra with bags of exercise equipment. They ring the bell and the door mysteriously opens. Unable to see anyone, they enter the house. They hear screaming from the top of the landing. They run upstairs to find the bedroom in a state of total disarray. The furniture has been smashed, objects are mysteriously swirling around in the air, arcane symbols appear in blood on the walls and at the centre of the room, strapped to a floating bed, is a man with white eyes, green pallid skin and a distending jaw filled with dagger-like teeth, cursing and spitting and vomiting out spiders. Cowering in the corner is the man who posted the notice. "I was expecting a priest," he sighed. "I really must work on my spelling."

The second trainer turns to the first: " No, not again! Remember when we answered that pilates ad and ended up walking the plank?!"

**What comes out of a wardrobe at 100 miles an hour?
A sports jacket.**

★ ★

A man goes to the gym and gets on an exercise machine. He begins running but after a few seconds he can't stop sneezing. He turns the machine off and talks to a member of staff.

"What's going on with that treadmill?"

"Oh, that's not a treadmill, that's a pepper mill!"

★ ★

A young, ambitious boxer has just finished his first bout, and sits down with his boxer friends, but his face is a real mess, covered in massive bruises and cuts and basically mashed up.

"You look a real state, Steve," one of them says.

"I know, I was terrible!" he said. "I need to get in better shape before my match next month, or I'll get destroyed."

"Have you tried skipping?" one of them suggested.

"Hmm, I'll give it a go," he said.

A month later the boxer sits down with his friends. This time his face is practically unmarked. He smiles at them all.

"You look much better Steve!" they all agree. "Did you try skipping?"

"I certainly did," he says. "And I think I'll skip the next match as well!"

EXERCISE

A man walks down the street when he spies an old friend that he hasn't seen for a couple of years. He remembers him as a rather portly and unfit young man, but now he's toned and lithe with a six-pack and bulging biceps. The man is amazed and approaches his old friend.

"Wow, Bill, what's your secret?"

"I murdered my wife's lover."

The man looks horrified. His friend suddenly smacks his forehead.

"Oh... you mean the gym thing!"

> **What's the fastest cake in the world?**
> **'Scone!**

Two women meet over coffee.

"I'm feeling so depressed right now," one of them says to the other.

"There are natural ways to deal with depression," her friend says. "You need to release some endorphins."

She nods at this advice.

A week later the woman bumps into her friend, who looks dishevelled but nevertheless excited. "What's happening?" she asks.

"Oh, I did what you suggested!" her friend replies. "I broke into the aquarium and released some endorphins! I'm going to Seaworld next – there's a killer whale there!"

Fairies

Cinderella is upset because the ugly sisters and her stepmother have gone to the ball and left her behind. All of a sudden, in a blue flash, a beautiful glowing fairy appears before her.

"Ah, Gingerella, it's me!"

"It's Cinderella, and who are you?"

"I'm your fairy godmother. And you shall go to the ball! I can cast any spell you want to help you meet your prince charming."

"Alright, first I need a beautiful ballgown."

"Your wish is my command, Binderella!" And – whoosh! – Cinderella is suddenly standing there in a fireman's outfit.

"Oh, sorry about that," says the fairy godmother. "Anyway, onto the shoes, Bongerella..."

"It's Cinderella! How about some delicate glass slippers, then?"

"No problem!" She waves her wand again and – whoosh! – Cinderella finds her feet encased in a pair of large bananas. "Oops, sorry about that again Dongerella."

"IT'S CINDERELLA!"

"Yeah, yeah. Now you probably need some kind of transport, right?"

"Yes," says Cinderella, "and please, make it some kind of elegant carriage."

The fairy godmother waves her wand at a pumpkin and – whoosh! – it transforms into a holiday bungalow, destroying the entire room.

Cinderella climbs out of the rubble: "Fairy godmother, what's going on?"

"I'm really sorry Winderella... I'm having trouble with my spelling."

* * * * * ★ ★ ★ * * * *

★ ★

One day a fairy is flying along and bumps into a bumblebee. The fairy says: "What kind of fairy are you?"

The bee, slightly offended, says in a superior tone, "I'm not a fairy, I'm a bombus terrestris.*"*

"Oh, you're a bumblebee!"

The bee was taken aback: "You speak Latin?"

"No, I just know that bumblebees are stuck-up chumps."

It's common knowledge that when forest fairies reach a certain age they are assigned a particular flower to look after. After one such ceremony, the young fairies gather together to compare their floral duties.

A tanned, blonde fairy produces a yellow flower with a big black centre: "I'm looking after sunflowers, apparently," he says.

Another fairy produces a many-petalled pink flower. "This is a carnation, that's my responsibility," she proudly declares.

One by one they produce their flowers – roses, chrysanthemums and pansies – until finally one much older-looking fairy is left and sheepishly produces a large white crusty loaf of bread from behind his back. The other fairies are confused. "What flower do you represent?" they cry.

"Self-raising flour," he shrugs. "I'm a late bloomer, apparently."

Fairytales

Once upon a time, there was a young woman who was nicknamed Cinderella by her stepmother and two ugly sisters. Everyday she was forced to work for them like an unpaid servant. One day, it was announced that there was to be an amazing ball at the palace and all the young maidens were sent invitations. But Cinderella's evil stepmother tore it up in front of her, telling her she would never be beautiful or elegant enough to attend.

   Cinderella was left weeping in the pantry when suddenly a wonderful glowing light appeared, and from it stepped an amazing apparition: "You come to me on the day of the Royal Ball. This is my gift to you," he said. "We'll put a horse's head in your stepmother's bed, you ain't gonna see them ugly sisters no more, we'll do a ram raid on the glass slipper shop, and make the Prince an offer he can't refuse."

   "Who are you?" she asked, stunned.

   "I'm the Fairy Godfather."

★ ★

Once upon a time, *Hansel and Gretel were left in the woods by their mother, who could no longer afford to feed them. Lost and frightened, they came across a house made of gingerbread and sweets.*

The door creaked open... to reveal one of the three little pigs!

"Quick, get inside, the wolf's coming!" He said desperately.

"Are you kidding?" said Gretel, "this won't stop him!"

"Of course it will," said the little pig. "He's diabetic!"

(Another little pig pops his head round the door to add: "And gluten intolerant!")

★ ★

Once upon a time in a magical land, there was a young thief named Aladdin. He was captured by an ancient sorcerer, who ordered him to enter a deep and mysterious cave full of riches beyond his wildest dreams and bring him only a single brass lamp.

The boy was confused but did as the sorcerer asked, travelled to the deepest part of the cave and found the lamp. He thought it looked a bit grubby so he gave it a rub... and one of the Three Little Pigs appeared!

"Quick, get in the lamp, the wolf's coming! He's got a brass allergy!"

Once upon a time in a town called Hamlyn, the people had a terrible plague of rats ruining their lives. They ate all the food, destroyed their houses and scared their children.

One day, a lone piper came to the town and promised to solve their problem. He asked only for 100 gold pieces, and the townspeople agreed. He lifted the pipe to his lips and began playing a merry tune, skipping and dancing his way out of town. As he danced, all the potatoes in the town suddenly leapt up and began dancing after him in a line.

"But what about the rats?" asked the mayor. "I thought he was the Pied Piper!"

His deputy shook his head. "Nah, that's the Maris Piper."

* * * ★ ★ ★ ★ ★ ★ ★ * * *

Once upon a time, a prince was riding through the vale when he saw a tall stone tower in the middle of the woods. From the window he heard beautiful singing and saw a maiden brushing a long cascade of golden hair.

"Sweet maiden, who has put you in this tower?" he asked.

"My wicked stepmother," she said. "You can save me, handsome prince."

She dropped her incredibly long tresses out of the window. "Quick, climb up my silken hair and I will be yours forever."

The prince quickly grabbed the hair and found it to be stronger than he thought. One step at a time, he slowly began to climb the tower. Before he reached halfway, he suddenly began scratching himself all over while dangling from one hand: "Sweet maiden, for some reason I'm itching all over!"

"Oh dear," sighed Rapunzel, "I guess that head-lice shampoo didn't work then."

* * * * * ★ ★ ★ ★ ★ * * *

Once upon a time, *Little Red Riding Hood was merrily skipping through the woods all the way to Grandma's house. When she arrived she found someone dressed in grandma's clothing in bed. At first she thought it was her beloved Grandma, but then she suddenly realised it was the Big Bad Wolf, although he seemed a bit startled and embarrassed to see her. She then noticed the wolf was actually tied to the bed.*

"Where's my Grandma?" Little Red Riding Hood exclaimed, and then opened the nearby wardrobe to find... Grandma... dressed as a wolf!

Grandma looked sheepish: "I told you never to visit me on Tuesdays!"

Once upon a time *two teeny tiny little girls were walking along in a town, looking for somewhere to stay. A kindly shopkeeper stopped in front of them, amazed at what he saw. "Why, you are no bigger than my hand! Do you seek refuge?"*

"We do, good sir," said the first girl. "My name is Thumbelina."

"Well, Thumbelina," said the man, "I make doll's houses, and I have a perfect little house where you can stay, with everything you would ever want in life."

"Buzz off, you old creep!" said the other little girl.

"What's wrong with her?" asked the shopkeeper.

"Sorry, sir," said Thumbelina. "That's my sister, Middlefingerlina."

"I wouldn't let that Cinderella play on my football team."
"Why not?"
"She keeps running away from the ball!"

What kind of pet did Aladdin have?
A flying car-pet.

What would you get if you crossed Bo Peep's littlest sheep
with a martial arts expert?
Lamb chops.

Fame

Two ordinary guys were walking along the road when an old man came up to one of them: "Excuse me, Mr Cruise? Tom Cruise? Would you mind signing this for my son? He's a big fan of yours and it'd mean so much to him."

"Sure, no problem," said the guy, signing the piece of paper and then walking away.

His friend gave him a funny look. "Why did you sign that? You're not Tom Cruise!"

"I know, but I didn't want to disappoint him. And I wouldn't want him to think Tom Cruise was rude."

"But when he takes your autograph back home to his son, he might look online and check it, then he'll know it's not a real autograph."

"Yeah, well... that's why I signed it Clint Eastwood!"

Andy Warhol said that in the future everyone would be famous for fifteen minutes. We now know that the fifteen minutes in question will be from noon to 12:15 p.m. on Thursday, 14 September, 2045.

A celebrity arrives at a film premiere. He starts to step onto the red carpet when he's stopped by a huge, burly security guard. "I'm sorry, the red carpet is only for A-list celebrities, sir."

"Right... so do I walk on this blue carpet?"

"No sir, we've got a new colour-grading system according to status. The blue carpet is for B-List celebrities."

"Not me?"

The security guard shakes his head.

"How about the yellow carpet?"

He shakes his head again: "C-list celebrities, sir – not you."

The celebrity is angry and confused: "So where the hell can I walk?"

The security guard looks the celebrity slowly up and down. Then he brings his walkie-talkie up to his lips: "Bert... we're gonna need some linoleum."

Fish

Alex had a terrible day fishing on the lake, sitting in the blazing sun all day without making a single catch. On his way home, he stopped at the fishmonger and ordered four rainbow trout. He told the fishmonger, "Pick four large ones out and throw them at me, will you?"

"Why do you want me to throw them at you?" he asked.

"So that I can tell my wife, in all honesty, that I caught them," said Alex.

"Okay, but I suggest that you take the salmon instead of the trout."

"Why's that?" asks Alex.

"Because your wife came in earlier today and said that if you came by, I should tell you to take salmon. That's what she'd like for supper tonight," replied the fishmonger with a grin.

A customer at Stingray Fishmongers marvelled at the owner's quick wit and intelligence. "Tell me, Simon, what makes you so smart?"

"I wouldn't share my secret with just anyone," Simon replies, lowering his voice so the other shoppers won't hear. "But since you're a good and faithful customer, I'll let you in on it. Fish heads. You eat enough of them, you'll be positively brilliant!"

"You sell them here?" the customer asks.

"Only £4 apiece," says Simon.

The customer buys three. A week later, he's back in the store complaining that the fish heads were disgusting and he isn't any smarter.

"You didn't eat enough," says Simon. This time the customer goes home with 20 more fish heads. Two weeks later, he's back and this time he's really angry.

"Hey, Simon," he complains, "you're selling me fish heads for £4 apiece when I can buy the whole fish for £2. You're ripping me off!"

"You see?" Simon tells him, "you're smarter already!"

After a Tuesday fishing on the river, Trevor is walking from the pier carrying two trout in a bucket. He is approached by a Water Conservation Officer, who asks him for his fishing licence.

"I wasn't fishing," Trevor replies, "and I didn't catch these brown trout. They are my pets. Every day I come down to the water and put these fish into the water and take them for a walk to the end of the pier and back. When I'm ready to go, I whistle and they jump back into the bucket and we go home."

The disbelieving officer reminds Trevor that it is illegal to fish without a licence. The fisherman turns to the warden: "If you don't believe me, then watch." He throws the trout back into the water.

"Right, now whistle to your fish and show me that they will jump out of the water and into the bucket," the warden demands.

Trevor turns to the officer and says, "What fish?"

I had a fish that could breakdance!
It could only do it on the carpet, though.
For 30 seconds. Once.

★ ★ ★ ★ ★ ★ ★ ★ ★ ★ ★ ★

Two fish in a tank. One says to the other, "How do we drive this thing?"

★ ★ ★ ★ ★ ★ ★ ★ ★ ★ ★ ★

Bill had always wanted to go ice fishing. He had read several books on the subject and, after getting all the necessary equipment together, he finally made his way out onto the ice.

As Bill began to make a circular cut in the ice, a sudden terrifying voice from above boomed out, "THERE ARE NO FISH UNDER THE ICE."

Startled, Bill moved further down the ice, poured himself a large coffee and began to cut yet another hole. Again, from the heavens, the voice bellowed, "THERE ARE NO FISH UNDER THE ICE."

Bill now became very concerned, so he moved way down to the opposite end of the ice and began to cut yet another hole. Once more the voice rang out: "THERE ARE NO FISH UNDER THE ICE."

Bill stopped, looked upwards and said, "Is that you, Lord?"

"NO," the voice replied, "THIS IS THE MANAGER OF THE ICE RINK!"

Cletus was telling his friend Jethro about his morning.

"Well, I went out fishin' but after a short time I ran out of worms. Then what did I see but a little crocodile with a frog in his mouth."

Jethro was amazed. "What'd you do? You run off?"

"Naw, frogs is good bait! I knew the crocodile couldn't bite me with the frog in his mouth, so I grabbed him right behind the head, took the frog, and put it in my bait bucket."

"Was he mad?"

"Sure he was! He bit me right on the foot! Luckily I was wearing my croc-proof boots."

Jethro's eyes were huge: "Wow! How'd you get away!"

Cletus nodded knowingly. "I grabbed my bottle of moonshine and I poured a little of it into his mouth. His eyes rolled back, he went limp and his jaw opened. Then I just released him into the lake and carried on fishing using the frog."

"You let it go? And you just stayed there?" Jethro exclaims, unbelieving. "What if it came back?"

"It did," said Cletus. "And this time it had two frogs..."

Flying

Three superheroes receive news of an emergency and are about to travel to the scene.

"How do you like to fly through the sky, Captain Flame?" asks the first. "I usually stick one arm out because it looks more dynamic."

"Ah, right. I like to stick two arms out in front. I find it gives me better control as I shoot through the sky. What about you, Thunderbolt?"

"I fly with my arms and legs tucked into my stomach as tight as possible and with my cape wrapped totally around me."

"Is that because it makes you more aerodynamic?"

"No, it's because it's flipping freezing!"

★★★★★★★★★★★★★★★★★★★★★★★

Before the Wright Brothers' successful first flight, every other attempt at manned flight was a disaster with crashing and lost lives. This was due to the involvement of the Wrong Brothers.

A bird is flying in formation when he notices the bird next to him is looking really exhausted, flapping away wildly.

"You know, you don't have to flap all the time," he says. "We're in an air current right now. If you just stick out your wings, you can glide for a long time."

"Oh, right. Thanks," says the bird, following his advice and looking much relieved.

"It's even easier than that!" says a bird lower than them. "I've had my wings tucked in for ages and I'm still whizzing along like nobody's business!"

"Yes, but you're on top of a train!"

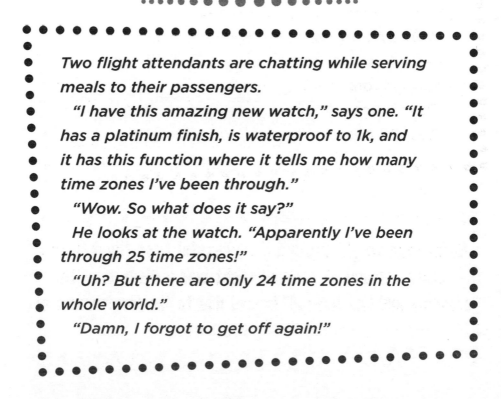

Two flight attendants are chatting while serving meals to their passengers.

"I have this amazing new watch," says one. "It has a platinum finish, is waterproof to 1k, and it has this function where it tells me how many time zones I've been through."

"Wow. So what does it say?"

He looks at the watch. "Apparently I've been through 25 time zones!"

"Uh? But there are only 24 time zones in the whole world."

"Damn, I forgot to get off again!"

With his plane about to take off, the pilot turns to the co-pilot, yawning. "You know, I've had a hell of a schedule recently. If you don't mind, can you take the lead today so I can get some shut-eye?"

"Uh... s-sure, okay."

"Don't worry! Just remember that this plane has a slightly different set of controls. See these three lights?" he says, indicating them on the board. His co-pilot nods."If the green light goes on, you need to flush ice out of the system. Just pull that lever."

"Okay."

"And if the blue light goes on, you need to equalise pressure in the cabin, so turn that dial until it reads 100."

"Right, got it."

"And if the red light goes on... well, you'd better wake me up."

The co-pilot gulps, but steels himself. They take off and the pilot settles down in the seat. First the green light goes off – the co-pilot is worried but pulls the lever. Then the blue light goes off and he turns the dial until it reads 100. But then, the red light starts flashing and beeping loudly. The co-pilot panics: "Oh my God, Oh my God, wake up, wake up!" he screams, shaking the pilot.

The pilot wakes and sees the red light. "Phew, you woke me just in time," he says. "My toasted cheese sandwich is done."

While barely tolerating their meals, two aeroplane passengers are chatting.

"Do you know why aeroplane food is so bad?" says one. "Not a lot of people know this, but all the companies that make aeroplane food are owned by car manufacturers. If the food was better, you see, more people would fly, and fewer people would buy cars. It's a conspiracy."

"Wow, really? So why is there so little legroom?"

"Because airline owners are slimeballs!"

★ ★

Three men disembark from a twelve-hour inter-continental flight.

"I don't know about you, John," says the first, "but I find jetlag really disorienting. I've got a killer technique to beat it. The instant I was on the flight I took two sleeping pills, chugged a glass of malt whisky and put my sleeping mask on. No problem."

The second man smiles. "I think my technique's much better. I don't touch alcohol or sleep. I just switch my watch to my home time zone, then read a travel book while continually taking small sips of water. Does the trick!"

The third man scoffed at this. "I've never had any problems with that. The second I was in my chair, I was fast asleep, snoring like a log. And as soon as the wheels hit the tarmac my eyes popped open, and I feel fresh as a daisy."

"Hang on," says the first man, "aren't you the pilot?"

Two World War Two fighter pilots are flying back from patrol.

"I say, Ginger, I can't wait to get back to Blighty," says the first pilot. "I'm heading straight for the officer's lounge, kick my bally feet up, pipe in the mouth, steaming cup of Darjeeling, and maybe a wink from Doris the tea lady! How about you, old sausage?"

"Well, once I've refuelled I'm going straight back up again."

"Blimey, we only just finished a five-hour sortie! But I don't blame you, old chap. Is it the thrill of the sky, zooming up into the blue, sticking your tongue out at old Mr Gravity and kissing the clouds?"

"No, it's not that."

"Ah, then it must be the exciting thought of combat, of some bally Jerry emerging from the clouds like a panther with murder in his eyes and bullets in his cannons."

"No, it's not that either... I dropped my spectacles over Normandy."

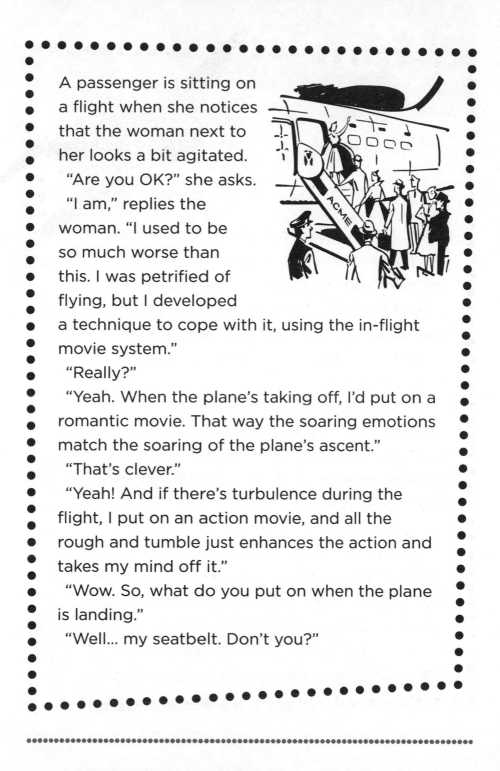

A passenger is sitting on a flight when she notices that the woman next to her looks a bit agitated.

"Are you OK?" she asks.

"I am," replies the woman. "I used to be so much worse than this. I was petrified of flying, but I developed a technique to cope with it, using the in-flight movie system."

"Really?"

"Yeah. When the plane's taking off, I'd put on a romantic movie. That way the soaring emotions match the soaring of the plane's ascent."

"That's clever."

"Yeah! And if there's turbulence during the flight, I put on an action movie, and all the rough and tumble just enhances the action and takes my mind off it."

"Wow. So, what do you put on when the plane is landing."

"Well... my seatbelt. Don't you?"

Food

A world-famous chef has a heart attack while choking on a fishbone. He finds himself in Hell, the Devil grinning and rubbing his claws together.

"Ah, a pleasure to meet you at last! We have good news and bad news. The good news is that we have devised a menu of tortures for you to match your own culinary prowess!" The man shivers with terror as the Devil continues, "We shall baste you in molten lava and then roast you gently over a coal fire, we shall plunge you into a sous vide tank of boiling hydrochloric acid, and prick you all over with an organically created artisanal trident."

"So... what's the bad news?" the terrified chef asks.

"You're not going to be able to get a table for at least two months."

What did the mayonnaise say to the refrigerator?
"Close the door! Can't you see I'm dressing?"

> **What's the difference between roast beef and pea soup?**
> **You can roast beef but you can't pee soup!**

★ ★ ★ ★ ★ ★ ★ ★ ★ ★ ★ ★ ★ ★ ★ ★ ★ ★ ★

Hugh and Priscilla were sitting down over coconut oil chai latte smoothies, discussing meals they'd had recently.

"I went to an amazing restaurant, the Romney. Their chef is Francois DeBotoloph. Ten Michelin stars, darling."

"What did you have?"

"They served a starfruit tagine foam with heritage aubergines, drizzled with Venezuelan lentil juice..."

"It must have been divine!"

"Yes, I photographed it and put it on Instagram, on my blog, my vlog, Pinterest, and I created a novelty Twitter account in its name."

"So how did it taste?"

"No idea, darling, I sent it back."

"Why?"

"It went cold."

★ ★ ★ ★ ★ ★ ★ ★ ★ ★ ★ ★ ★ ★ ★ ★ ★ ★ ★

* * * * * ★ ★ ★ * * *

A group of chefs are busy putting together orders for a high profile restaurant when the head chef comes in, his face ashen. "Heston Blumenthal has just come in with a group of his friends... by which I mean Jamie Oliver, Yotam Ottolenghi, Gordon Ramsey and Nigella Lawson." The chefs begin to panic. Theirs is a well-regarded restaurant, but how could they possibly please such a table?

"What have they ordered?" asks the sous chef.

"That's just it," he says, "they've all asked for baked beans on toast!"

The chefs look at each other, confused.

"That's not on the menu," says the sous chef. "I'm not even sure we have any baked beans or bread?"

"Well, have someone nip over to the cornershop to pick up a loaf of sliced white and a half a dozen tins."

But the head chef needs to know what's happening. He goes over to the table: "Ladies and gentlemen, I need to know why you've all asked for beans on toast! This is a three-star restaurant, we have a diverse menu of award-winning dishes. Is this some kind of insult?"

Heston holds up his hand to quieten the chef: "Not at all! As you know, we're all famous chefs who spend every day making and tasting high-quality, exotic dishes. After a while you just get a bit sick of it. So while we're all out we thought we'd go for something simple and normal – not fancy, just basic and satisfying."

The chef is appeased. "I understand," he replies. "So what would you like to drink?"

"Carbonated Moldovian weasel sweat."

* * * * * ★ ★ ★ ★ ★ * * * *

A man in a diner says to the waitress: "What flavours of ice-cream do you have?"

"Vanilla, salted caramel and chocolate," answered the waitress in a hoarse whisper.

Trying to be sympathetic, the customer asked, "Do you have laryngitis?"

"No...." replied the new waitress with some effort, "just... erm... vanilla, salted caramel and chocolate."

Edgar invites his friend Chuck over for a barbecue. He serves him up a bun full of tender, sizzling meat slathered in barbecue sauce and watches while Chuck tucks in.

"I'm so glad you came," Edgar says. "I've been meaning to share my new culinary discovery with someone."

"What's that?" says Chuck with his mouth full.

"Roadkill cooking! I read this article about it, it's amazing! Last week I found a dead possum by the side of the road, shaved and tenderised it – delicious with a honey mustard sauce! And then on Friday there was this skunk just by the interstate, I parboiled it and did this lovely tomato glaze..."

Chuck peers at the bun he's holding. "So ... what's this?"

Edgar grins. "Chicken!"

Chuck looks confused. "You found a chicken as roadkill? That must have taken some effort."

Edgar nodded. "It sure did. I chased that damn thing round my neighbour's garden in my pickup truck for 20 minutes!"

> **How many chefs does it take to change a garlic bulb?**

* ⋆ ⋆ ⋆ ⋆ ★ ★ ★ ⋆ ⋆ ⋆ ⋆

"I went to the farmer's market the other day!"
"Really, what did you get?"
"Two farmers, a stable boy, and a bag full of sheepdogs!"

⋆ ⋆ ⋆ ⋆ ★ ★ ★ ★ ⋆ ⋆ ⋆ ⋆

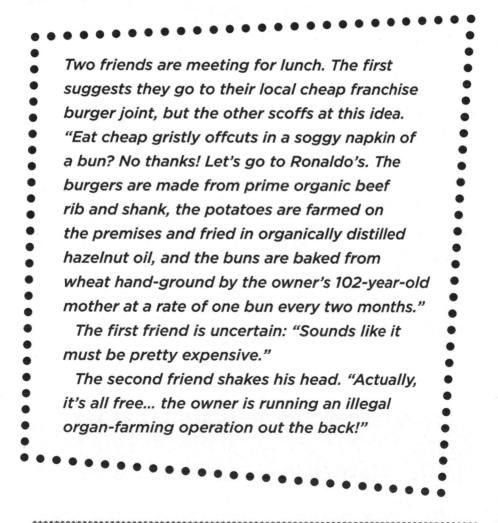

Two friends are meeting for lunch. The first suggests they go to their local cheap franchise burger joint, but the other scoffs at this idea. "Eat cheap gristly offcuts in a soggy napkin of a bun? No thanks! Let's go to Ronaldo's. The burgers are made from prime organic beef rib and shank, the potatoes are farmed on the premises and fried in organically distilled hazelnut oil, and the buns are baked from wheat hand-ground by the owner's 102-year-old mother at a rate of one bun every two months."

The first friend is uncertain: "Sounds like it must be pretty expensive."

The second friend shakes his head. "Actually, it's all free... the owner is running an illegal organ-farming operation out the back!"

A journalist is called at work by a chef friend in need of solace.

"What's up, Kenneth?" the journalist asks.

"Well, you know we had the grand opening of my new restaurant last week?"

"Oh yeah, what kind of food does it serve again?"

His friend chides him: "It doesn't exactly serve food, it provides a gastronomic assault on your organoleptic senses. Modern cuisine is as much a science as an art, I have a sous vide *isolation tank*, a sauce distillation vacuum chamber, not to mention the macrobiotic centrifuge..."

"So what was the problem?"

"We had to close on the first night?"

"Why was that?"

"The chip pan caught fire."

★ ★

More and more people are turning to street food nowadays. And once you've got rid of the gravel and cigarette butts it can be really tasty.

Friendship

Me and my friend Dave, we're so close, we always finish each other's sentences. I wouldn't mind, but he's just gone down for 15 years for armed robbery.

A man walks home from a bar when he comes across a friend on his hands and knees under a street light, feeling around.

"Are you okay?" he asks.

"No, I lost my car keys!"

"Alright, no problem, I'll help." And he gets on his hands and knees and joins in the search. After about 15 minutes he asks his friend, "Are you sure this is where you lost them?"

"No," his friend replies, "I lost them further down the street, but the light's better here."

> A good friend is always there with a shoulder to cry on. A best friend is always there with a bottle of alcohol, a huge chocolate cake and a sitcom box set.

A group of four friends decide to go bowling. None of them are particularly good at it, except for one very ambitious and sporty individual who time after time scores a perfect strike. They can't figure out how she's managing to do it. She doesn't seem to be throwing the ball very precisely, or have any special technique, but she manages to get a strike without fail.

"How are you doing it, Paula?" asks one of the friends.

Paula looks back and forth conspiratorially and then leans in close and whispers: "On my way in here, I saw the owner talking to his son. Apparently the foundations of the building have started to collapse on the west side. It could all crash into the basement at any time!"

"Oh my God, seriously?!"

"Yeah, so I figured that if I direct my ball over to the east, the building's natural slope would direct it right down the middle."

Paula's friend shakes his head. "But... this is incredibly dangerous! We've got to get out of here! Why didn't you tell us all sooner, just so you could win a stupid bowling game?"

"No! What kind of friend do you think I am?" Paula replies. "I'm actually waiting for the pool table to be free!"

A woman was walking home one day when she saw a cat and a dog in a garden playing together completely innocently, seemingly totally happy with the arrangement. She noted a man standing nearby.

"Are you their owner?" she asked.

"They live in my house, if that's what you mean," the man answered sardonically.

"I just wanted to say that I think it's so sweet to see a dog and a cat who are friends like that," the woman said. "Did they grow up together?"

"Nope!" replied the man. "It's just that the dog doesn't know what a cat is. He's always lived in a neighbourhood with only dogs, so when we adopted the cat he assumed it was another dog."

"So does the cat know what dogs are?" the woman asked.

"That's the strange thing," said the man. "The cat grew up wild in a place with a lot of scary, vicious dogs. He should have been terrified, but they get on like a house on fire."

"That is weird," says the woman.

Then the cat turns to the woman and says, "No, what's really weird is that he thinks Taylor Swift is better than Adele!"

A man goes to a psychiatrist, trembling and sweating, and tells him he has a serious problem: "Every time I go to bed I think there's somebody under it... I can't stop thinking about it, I can't sleep, I think I'm going insane!"

"Just put yourself in my hands for one year," says the psychiatrist. "You'll come talk to me three times a week and we should be able to get rid of those fears."

"So how much do you charge?" asks the man.

"£75 per visit," says the doctor.

"I'll sleep on it and if needed I'll come back to you," the man replies.

Six months later, the psychiatrist sees the same man on the street, and he seems to be doing well. "Why didn't you come to see me about those fears you were having?" he asked.

"Well, £75 a visit three times a week for a year is an awful lot of money! A friend of mine cured me for £10. I was so happy to have saved all that money that I went and bought myself a new 4 × 4."

"And how, may I ask, did your friend cure you?" asked the psychiatrist, with more than a touch of scepticism.

"He told me to cut the legs off the bed – there's definitely nobody under there now!"

Two old friends, Albert and Morris, went to the state fair every year. Each year, Morris would say to his friend, "Albert, I'd like to ride in that helicopter." Albert would always reply, "I know, Morris, but that helicopter ride is $50. And $50 is $50."

One year at the fair, Morris said to Albert, "I'm 85 years old. If I don't ride that helicopter today, I might never get another chance." As ever, Albert replied, "Morris that helicopter ride is $50. And $50 is $50."

The pilot overheard the friends and said, "Fellas, I'll make you a deal. I'll take the both of you for a ride. If you can stay quiet for the entire ride and don't say a single word, I won't charge you a penny! But if you say just one word it's $50."

Morris and Albert agreed, and up they went. The pilot did all kinds of fancy manoeuvres, but not a word was heard. He did his daredevil tricks over and over again, but still not a word. When they landed, the pilot turned to Morris and said, "Wow! I did everything I could to get you to yell out, but you didn't. I'm impressed!"

"Well, to tell you the truth," Morris replied, "I almost said something when Albert fell out, but – you know – $50 is $50!"

Gambling

Every day, Gladys Thorpe would come into the Pahrump Nugget Casino, sit down at the fourth slot machine in the seventh row, and spend almost the whole day putting quarter after quarter into it. She did this for twenty years, never missing a day, not even attending her daughter's wedding.

She never won. Until one day, Gladys's machine suddenly lit up with three golden bars, and with whooping sirens and flashing lights deposited half a million dollars' worth of coins right into her lap.

The manager of the casino was there in a flash, and called the local press who sent a reporter to interview her. "So now you've won the jackpot, what are you going to do?" the reporter asked.

"Well..." said Gladys, pointing to her left, "...I think I'll try that machine over there."

How many gamblers does it take to change a lightbulb? 4. No, wait, 6. Hang on, the smart money's on 10....

A guy gets home from work one night and hears a voice. The voice tells him, "Quit your job, sell your house, take your money, go to Vegas." The man is disturbed at what he hears and ignores the voice.

The next day when he gets home from work, the same thing happens. The voice tells him, "Quit your job, sell your house, take your money, go to Vegas." Again the man ignores the voice, though he is very troubled.

Every day, day after day, the man hears the same voice when he gets home from work. "Quit your job, sell your house, take your money, go to Vegas." Each time the man hears the voice he becomes increasingly upset. Finally, after two weeks, he succumbs to the pressure. He quits his job, sells his house, takes his money and heads to Vegas.

The moment the man gets off the plane in Vegas, the voice tells him, "Go to Harrah's." So, he hops in a cab and rushes over to Harrah's. As soon as he sets foot in the casino, the voice tells him, "Go to the roulette table." The man does as he is told. At the table, the voice tells him, "Put all your money on 17." Nervously, the man cashes in his money for chips and then puts them all on 17. The dealer wishes the man good luck and spins the roulette wheel.

Around and around the ball goes. The man anxiously watches the ball as it slowly loses speed until finally it settles into number... 21.

The voice says, "Damn!"

GAMBLING

//

★ ★

A group of men are in a pub near a stadium, watching the preamble of a football match on a big screen.

"Alright, lads, this is going to be a tricky one, but we can bet on a lot of things in this match. How much extra time, how many throw-ins and injuries there'll be, how many goals will be scored, how many yellow cards there'll be."

A man at the bar interrupts. "You know what, I can tell you that there will be exactly eight yellow cards in this match. If you make that bet, I'll split the money with you."

The man is sceptical: "I'm sorry, mate, but there's no way you could know that."

"Sure I can. After all, I'm the referee."

A man is in an addiction clinic, talking to the chief psychiatrist.

"I'm sorry but I don't think there's anything further I can do for you," he says. "You consistently refuse to engage with the process. I think without more from you you'll never break your crippling gambling addiction."

The man seems genuinely remorseful. "I'm sorry, Doctor, but I think I'm ready to turn a corner, I think I could now go a whole week without gambling."

The doctor says, "I really don't think you could."

The man says, "Wanna bet?"

A man shows his friend his favourite online poker website.

"I don't get how you can play poker online," his friend says. "How can you judge whether the other players are bluffing if you can't see their faces."

"I've got a technique for that!" the guy says. "I look at their profile names and then I imagine them in my head. For example, JohnnyRed23, I picture him as a sort of 1920s gambler, wearing braces and with striking red hair. Then I can see his face."

"That's clever. What about LaserLindaXX?"

"I see her as a sort of mad scientist, short blond hair, big glasses and laser focused."

"And Happy_Hands_Harry?"

"He's sort of a big wide guy, like a wrestler, huge smile with big hands wearing white gloves."

"OK. What about AlanTheGuyWhoAlways BluffsUnlessHeGetsSomethingBiggerThanA PairAndYouCanTellHe'sBluffingWhenHeStarts UsingTooManyCapitalLetters?"

"To be honest, I can't really get a read on him."

Two greyhounds are on a course waiting for the latest heat of the greyhound derby. One of them turns to the other and says:

"You know what, Jim? Have you ever seen the front of the rabbit?"

"As it happens, Tony, no, no I haven't, it's always too far ahead."

"In fact, we've never caught it. Does that ever wind you up?"

"It does!" says Jim. "But what can we do?"

"OK, here's my idea. I'll run after the rabbit, and you run the other way around the course and try and get it from the front. That way, at least one of us has to catch it, right?" Jim nods enthusiastically.

Seconds later, the announcer starts the race: "And they're off! Clever Tony in the lead there, followed by White Mist, and... oh my word, Lucky Jim has leapt the traps and is heading in completely the wrong direction! So it's Clever Tony to win by a mile, and Lucky Jim disqualified for being a silly boy."

An hour later, two greyhounds are on a course waiting for the semi-finals of the greyhound derby. One of them turns to the other and says: "You know what, Patrick?"

Gardening

★ ★ ★ ★ ★ ★ ★ ★ ★ ★ ★ ★ ★ ★

Every year Stuart and Diana, two particularly competitive neighbours with adjoining vegetable patches, took part in a squash-growing competition. Whoever's squash was biggest by the end of summer had to give the other a big cash payout.

Every year the two gardeners resorted to ever more elaborate techniques to try and ensure their squash was the mightiest – from sun lamps and magnifying greenhouses to cow's manure and all types of rotting vegetables. Every year, however, Diana won.

Stuart found this very frustrating and became even more determined to beat her. So through a series of connections he managed to get hold of some actual nuclear waste and, with great trepidation, dug it around his embryonic squash inside a lead-lined greenhouse.

On the day of reckoning, the two watched avidly as their squashes were measured. But it was a mere formality – Stuart's was clearly almost twice the size of Diana's.

"Well," Diana conceded, "you've won. Your squash is clearly bigger. I have no idea how you did it."

And Stuart's squash piped up, "I'd tell you, love, but he's promised me half the money."

★ ★ ★ ★ ★ ★ ★ ★ ★ ★ ★ ★ ★ ★ ★

• • • • • • • • • • • • • • • • • •

What does a plumber grow in his garden?
Leeks!

• • • • • • • • • • • • • • • • •

Janet is always amazed by her next door neighbour's garden. It's filled with tulips from end to end and dotted with garden gnomes all around. Yet she never sees her neighbour gardening. One morning, spotting her neighbour leaving for work, curiosity gets the better of her and she goes over to talk to him.

"Excuse me, your garden always looks so lovely with those tulips, but I never see you out there. How do you do it?"

The man looks around shiftily. "Okay," he whispers, "I'll tell you the truth. It's the gnomes. Every night they come to life. They plant and water all the flowers themselves!"

"That's incredible!" the woman says. "But have you ever asked them to plant anything other than tulips?"

The man moves to open his car door, using the tulips that once were his hands: "If you want to have that conversation with them, you go right ahead!"

> **What does Doctor Who grow in his garden?**
> **Thyme and relatively delicious spice.**

A group of moles have been searching for months for a garden in which they can live in peace. Everywhere they go is either dry and lifeless or filled with humans who try to capture and poison them.

One day, one of the moles comes back from a scouting trip excited and out of breath: "I've just found the perfect garden! It's covered with luscious bright green grass and it even has loads of holes and tunnels there already – we don't even have to dig!"

The moles are amazed. "Are there are any humans there?" asks one.

"That's the thing," says the scout. "There are, but they all ignore you, they're all doing something else!"

The moles are uncertain but excited. "Not just that," he carries on, "it even has little houses we can live in! And a windmill, and clowns to entertain us, slides and seesaws – even little pyramids! It's amazing!" The moles are thrilled.

"There's just one thing," says the scout, producing a golf ball. "Don't try to eat any of these eggs, you'll break your teeth..."

"Did you know," said one gardener to the other, "that I know the names of all the plants in my garden in Latin?" The other gardener shook his head. "That's not that impressive, Lucius Volcatius Tullus."

A man is always impressed by his neighbour's garden, which manages to be luscious, green and verdant all year round, whereas his own garden is a wilderness where plants seemingly refuse to grow. One day he asks his neighbour how he manages to have such an amazing garden. "It's simple really," his neighbour opines, "I just water very lightly, very minimal trimming, and of course, dust all the plastic twice a week."

What do sumo wrestlers grow in their gardens?
Squash.

A man is having a drink with his friend on his patio in the back garden. He points to an area of soil at the end of the garden. "Do you know what?" he says, "when I was nine years old I planted a jelly bean in the soil right there. Every week since then I've watered the soil and put compost down, and yet a jellybean tree has never grown there!"

His friend gives him a very funny look. "Are you nuts? Of course a jellybean tree has never grown there. Everyone knows that in this soil you can only grow candy cane bushes and gumdrop vines."

What do cosmetic surgeons grow in their gardens?
Tulips.

Why are weeds called weeds when they're so tough to get rid of?

* * * * * ★ ★ ★ * * * *

Everyone thinks Adam and Eve were thrown out of the garden of Eden for eating the Apple of Knowledge, but they were actually thrown out for not weeding the azalea beds.

* * * * * ★ ★ ★ * * * *

What do chickens grow in their gardens? Eggplant.

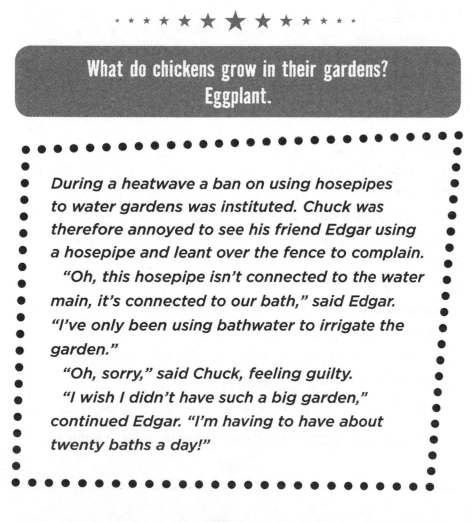

During a heatwave a ban on using hosepipes to water gardens was instituted. Chuck was therefore annoyed to see his friend Edgar using a hosepipe and leant over the fence to complain.

"Oh, this hosepipe isn't connected to the water main, it's connected to our bath," said Edgar. "I've only been using bathwater to irrigate the garden."

"Oh, sorry," said Chuck, feeling guilty.

"I wish I didn't have such a big garden," continued Edgar. "I'm having to have about twenty baths a day!"

A little girl is helping her grandfather dig up potatoes in the garden.

"This is really hard work, Granddad!" she says. He nods and carries on digging. "And I don't know why you buried them in the first place."

★ ★

> Mary, Mary, quite contrary, how does your garden grow? "Actually, it's not a garden, it's a small paved area with a water feature. And my name's not Mary, it's Amanda."

Two friends decided to go to see a supposed psychic medium performing at their local theatre. The room was packed and an expectant hush fell over the room as the performer came onto the stage. He put his hands to his head and narrowed his eyes.

"I'm receiving a message... a name... someone beginning with an N... Nigel? No, Nathaniel!"

Suddenly a potted aspidistra in the front row shouted, "That was the name of my grandfather!"

The medium peered at the aspidistra and said, "Well, if you'd please come up onto the stage."

One of the friends was amazed. "That's incredible!" she said.

Her friend rolled her eyes. "Come on, that's clearly a plant."

Golf

As a funeral cortège passes by a golf course, a golfer on one of the greens stops playing and stands to attention, his hat held over his heart as the hearse passes. Then he goes back to lining up his putt. His playing partner remarks how that was the nicest gesture he'd ever seen, to show such respect for the dead. The first golfer sinks his putt, turns to him and says, "Well, she was a good wife for sixteen years."

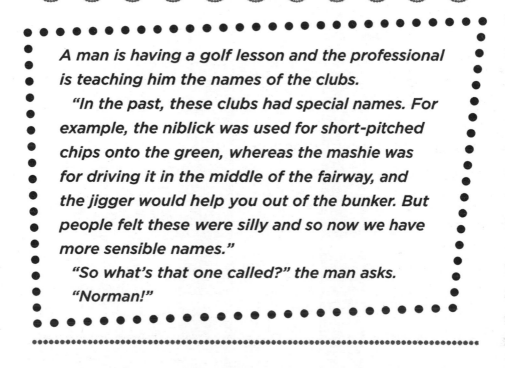

A man is having a golf lesson and the professional is teaching him the names of the clubs.

"In the past, these clubs had special names. For example, the niblick was used for short-pitched chips onto the green, whereas the mashie was for driving it in the middle of the fairway, and the jigger would help you out of the bunker. But people felt these were silly and so now we have more sensible names."

"So what's that one called?" the man asks.

"Norman!"

* * * * * * ★ ★ ★ * * * *

Henry moves into a new area. On the day of his arrival he is visited by the local priest. "You're going to love it around here, this is a wonderful community," says the priest. "Plus it has a fantastic golf course," he adds with a wink. "Do you play?"

"I do, as a matter of fact. We must set up a match," says Henry.

The following Sunday after mass they meet at the golf course and set off. At the first hole, Henry puts his ball down, takes a massive swing at it and completely misses the ball! He glares at the tee.

"Damn! I missed!" Henry shouts.

"Henry, I know that you are frustrated but I must ask that you do not use blasphemous profanities," says the priest. Henry apologises profusely.

Henry manages to get the ball onto the fairway. On his next turn he squares up, fixes his eye on the ball, brings his club back in a calculated arc, and as he swings... somehow completely misses the ball again. "Damn! I missed!" he shouts again.

The priest glares at him. "Henry, you really must not use any more blasphemous profanities, it is an affront to the Lord!" Once again Henry is deeply apologetic.

Henry collects himself and eventually manages to get the ball onto the green, three inches from the hole. This time he plants his feet, lines up, putts the ball... and watches as it trickles past the hole to the left. "Damn! I missed!" he shouts yet again.

The priest fixes Henry with a cold hard stare. "Henry, if you blaspheme one more time, I am certain that the Lord himself will strike you down for your wickedness!" Henry is shocked by this suggestion and is cowed into silence.

He carefully walks over to the ball, confident of getting it into the hole. But in his nervous excitement he hits it far too hard and it goes sailing over the hole back into a bunker. "Damn! I missed!" he screams, throwing his golf club in a fit of pique.

Suddenly a rumbling sound of thunder is heard in the heavens, and out of nowhere a massive bolt of lightning shoots down from the sky, incinerating the priest.

A great voice booms out, "DAMN, I MISSED!"

* * * * ★ ★ ★ ★ * * * *

Two golfers in the clubhouse are having a post-match drink. One of them remarks, "You know, I just realised that golf spelled backwards is flog!"
His friend says, "The way you play it, it's park backwards!"

> Mark Twain is often quoted as saying that golf is "a good walk spoiled." Personally, I think people who go for walks are just golfers without any balls.

> **Why did the golfer change his socks?**
> **Because there was a hole in one.**

A golfer stands on the sixteenth tee of a par-four hole. He takes a mighty swing at the ball, only to see it slice its way over the trees.

He continues his round without even bothering to look for it. Later, while he's enjoying a post-match drink at the bar, a serious-looking police officer enters the room. "Did anyone in the clubhouse hit a ball over the trees at the sixteenth?" he enquires loudly.

Everyone in the bar looks at each other. After a moment's thought our golfer comes forward: "I think I did, officer. Is there a problem?"

"Did you notice the pall of smoke rising from behind the trees?" The man looks out of the window and nods. "Well," the officer continues, "that's a petroleum tanker on fire. Your ball hit a passing cyclist on the head and he swerved in front of it, causing it to smash into a tree and explode!" The golfer looks aghast. "I'm afraid it doesn't end there. The fireball from the tanker has ignited a hospital. They are evacuating the staff and patients as we speak."

The man is now on his knees in despair. "What can I do? What on earth can I do?" he cries in anguish.

The police officer adopts a golfing stance and says, "Well, if you move your left leg back slightly and reduce your swing a little...."

Phyllis and Gertrude are playing golf. Phyllis is trying to blast her way out of the rough, but puts too much club on the ball and it ends up in the woods. "That ball's gone, then," Gertrude sighs.

"*Au contraire*," says Phyllis. They venture into the woods together and Phyllis gives a little whistle. They hear a whistle back. Phyllis keeps whistling and eventually they find the ball under some leaves, whistling away.

"That's brilliant," says Gertrude.

"That's nothing," replies Phyllis. "The ball glows in the dark too, so you can find it at night. And if it falls into a water trap, it inflates a raft, bobs right to the top and a tiny motor propels it back to the shore!"

"Amazing!" says Gertrude. "Where can I get one?"

"No idea," says Phyllis, "I just found it!"

★ ★

A billionaire takes his first golf lesson. Standing on the first tee, the club professional explains to him how to get started.

"Right, what you have to do is tee off."

"What do I need for that?" the billionaire asks.

"A driver," comes the reply.

As the billionaire starts to walk off, the club professional asks him where he's going. "To get my driver," he retorts. "I left him in the limo!"

Hackers

A young man was idly poking around various subroutines and accidentally hacked into the Pentagon. He suddenly found that he had total control of America's entire nuclear arsenal.

"This is a big moment," he thought. "I have the power of life and death over an entire continent... no, the whole world! If I launched even a single attack the chain reaction of counter-attack upon counter-attack would be a domino effect of destruction so awesome that civilisation itself would cease to be!

"Alternatively, if I were to shut everything down, I could herald a new age of peace, a world where we no longer lived in terror of annihilation, because all the nuclear weaponry had been eradicated!"

Then he remembered he was a teenager, and programmed the missiles to bomb his school in the shape of the word "FART".

★ ★

There are three types of computer hacker:
  White hat hackers, who hack things ethically.
  Black hat hackers, who hack things maliciously.
  And wide-brimmed strawhat covered in fake flowers and butterflies hackers, who hack things very carefully because they can barely see the screen.

Two computer hackers had known each other for many years. Over time, resentment and envy had grown between them and they had now become bitter rivals. From time to time, they would try to hack each other's systems, but as each was as paranoid as the other they always had a swathe of counter-intrusion software in place and neither one ever succeeded.

One day, however, one of the hackers somehow managed to get into the other's system. He didn't expect it to work, but just tried it as a joke, yet suddenly, he was able to see his rival's entire system laid bare for him to manipulate – hidden files... emails... all his devices....

Suddenly, the hacker felt paranoid. What if this was the plan all along? To let him into his system, then somehow use it to hack him back? That's exactly the kind of sneaky thing his rival – well, both of them, in fact – would do! No way would he fall into that trap!

But then he hesitated again. What if this was for real? He couldn't pass up an opportunity like this! So he set about destroying everything! Then he realised that his worst fear was true. It was a trap and his rival was destroying all their files as well.

Eventually, with both of their servers up in smoke, the hackers met up. Sitting on opposite sides of a table they glared.

"You destroyed everything," said the first.

"You destroyed all my stuff too!" said the second.

"You know what?" said the first. "I don't know why we got married in the first place!"

///

A man goes to the doctor and says, "I've got this terrible tickle in my throat."

"That's normal for hay fever season," says the doctor.

"Sure," continues the man, "but the weird thing is that I tried to clear my throat and suddenly found my computer was logged into a secret government database. I did it again, and this time my computer had got into the Vatican's archives."

"Mmhm" says the doctor, and writes down on his pad "HACKING COUGH".

• • • • • • • ● ● ● ● • • • •

A woman goes through a bad break-up and wants to get revenge on her girlfriend. She goes online and finds a community of hackers and solicits one of them to help her get vengeance.

"I want you to go into all of her social media accounts and write that she's a wonderful person with great charisma. In fact, rewrite all of her posts so that everyone loves her and thinks she's brilliant."

"Okay," said the hacker, "but wouldn't it be a better revenge if you made her look really awful in all her social media posts? Like, unpleasant and racist?"

The woman shakes her head: "She already looks really terrible in her social media posts. She is a big mean racist."

"Then why do you want me to change them?"

"So she loses all her friends!"

A criminal decided to hack into the mainframe of a bank and transfer millions of dollars into his own account. He needed the password of the bank's CEO, but decided it would be easier to try to figure it out than to spend months trying to break into confidential encrypted files.

He first tried all the obvious ones like 123456 or password1, but nothing would work. This CEO was no idiot.

He then tried the name of the CEO's wife, his parents, his kids, his dog, anyone connected to him even vaguely – even his cousin's dentist's roommate at college. Nothing.

He tried things the CEO enjoyed: Shakespeare, opera, the New York Mets, fillet steak... Still nothing.

In frustration he snapped. He found out where the CEO lived, broke into his house and held him at gunpoint tied to a chair.

"I've had it," he yelled. "TELL ME YOUR PASSWORD!"

"I can't, I can't!" This CEO was incredible, thought the criminal. Not only was his password impossible to guess, but even with a gun held to his head he wouldn't give up the information.

The CEO started crying. "I can't because... I changed it two months ago and I don't remember what it bloody is!"

Hairdressers

A young man goes to see his barber. "I need advice," he said. "You see, for two years I parted my hair on the right. But nobody wanted to go out with me. Then I tried parting it on the left for two years. Still no joy. Then I tried parting it down the middle. Guess what? Nothing happened. What can you suggest?"

"Have you tried growing out your fringe?" the hairdresser says.

"No, how long should I have it?"

"Down to your chin should do the trick."

A man arrives in a new town and needs a haircut. He sees lots of different hairdressers, but one in particular catches his eye because it has the cheapest rates he's ever seen. He goes in and asks the hairdresser why his cuts are so cheap.

"I'll tell you a secret, sir," the hairdresser says. "Once you've been in my chair, you'll never need another haircut again!"

"That's fantastic." says the man. "Do your best, Mr Todd!"

A young man planned to open a hairdressing salon and visited his local barber shop to get tips on how to set himself up. He asked about mirrors, chairs, and all of the various equipment. Then he pointed to the big jar of blue liquid where the combs were kept.

"How do I go about gettin' some of that?" he asked.

"You mean Barbicide?" said the barber.

The young man considered this, then pulled out a gun and shot him. "Okay, and then I just take it?"

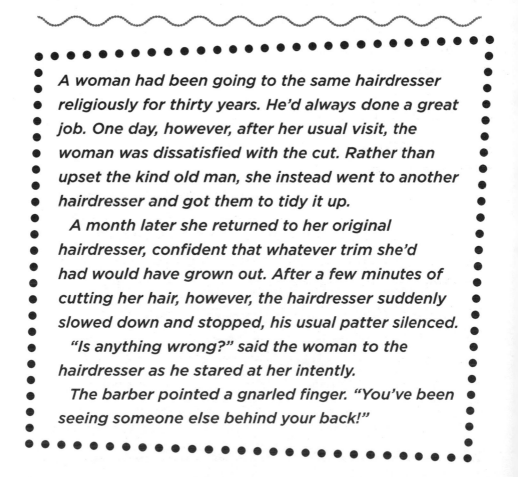

A woman had been going to the same hairdresser religiously for thirty years. He'd always done a great job. One day, however, after her usual visit, the woman was dissatisfied with the cut. Rather than upset the kind old man, she instead went to another hairdresser and got them to tidy it up.

A month later she returned to her original hairdresser, confident that whatever trim she'd had would have grown out. After a few minutes of cutting her hair, however, the hairdresser suddenly slowed down and stopped, his usual patter silenced.

"Is anything wrong?" said the woman to the hairdresser as he stared at her intently.

The barber pointed a gnarled finger. "You've been seeing someone else behind your back!"

HAIRDRESSERS

* * * * * ★ ★ ★ ★ * * * *

A woman with beautiful blonde hair goes into her hairdressers and asks for it to be coloured.

"I'd like to be as red as possible, please." The hairdresser happily complies, tinting it a rich auburn. The woman looks at it in the mirror and shakes her head.

"No, brighter please. Not red enough." The hairdresser shrugs and tints it an intense titian. The woman shakes her head again.

"No, much redder, please!"

The hairdresser rolls up her sleeves and dyes the hair a bright tomato red. The woman nods her head.

"Perfect! So red that it'll stop traffic!"

"Why do you want to stop traffic?" asks the hairdresser.

"Oh, because I'm a lollipop lady!"

* * * * * ★ ★ ★ ★ * * * *

Juliet Capulet has a secret assignation with her beloved Romeo, and wants to look her most gorgeous. So she gets her servant to attend to her hair. The servant tries all kinds of different styles but none of them seem to satisfy her – from braids to a bun to a ponytail. Eventually she just parts it down the middle. Juliet immediately bursts into tears. The servant is upset, but Juliet sobs: "I'm so happy!"

  "Why is that, my lady?"

  "Because partings are such sweet sorrow!"

A woman is having her hair cut, but the hairdresser seems really nervous. Suddenly, the scissors slip and the hairdresser cuts the woman's ear clean off! The woman immediately claps her hand to the side of her head, blood dribbling through her fingers.

"OH MY GOD, WHAT HAVE YOU DONE?" the woman shouts.

"I'm so sorry!" says the stylist. "Don't worry, I've had training about this, I know exactly what to do!"

With one swift snip she cuts the other ear clean off. "There you go, now it's symmetrical!"

★ ★

A man goes along to an audition for a barbershop quartet. They need a new baritone for their group. Before hearing him sing, they tell him, "I hope you realise we're considered the Number 1 barbershop group in the country. We're meticulous and painstaking in our method and we demand perfection."

After nailing the audition, they ask him if he'd like the job. "That's great," he says. "Just out of curiosity, what happened to your original baritone."

"Well, we're all actual barbers. Anyway, he joined the army and let's just say... he took too many short cuts."

HAIRDRESSERS

A woman goes into a salon to get a perm. The hairdresser washes her hair, wraps it in curlers and adds the necessary liquid. After a while, it's removed and her hair is carefully blow-dried. Delighted with her new bouncing locks, she skips out of the hairdressers. Moments later she returns, her hair as flat as a pancake.

"What happened? This is supposed to be a perm!"

"Sorry," says the receptionist, "the girl who did it is a temp."

★★★★★★★★★★★★★★★★★★★★★★★

A hairdresser is talking to her client. "How would you like me to style your hair today?"

"Well, I've always wanted to look like Keira Knightley. Do you think you could do that?"

"No problem at all!" The hairdresser exclaims, and sets to work.

With quick snips of her scissors she cuts the hair shorter and shorter, then suddenly whips out a set of clippers and shaves the woman completely bald.

"Oh my God, what the hell have you done! I said Keira Knightley!" screams the woman.

"I know!" says the hairdresser. " And this is exactly how he has it in *Fast and Furious*!"

Hamsters

Kirsty has always wanted to go to Spain and take part in the running of the bulls in Pamplona. But just as she's about to book the tickets her friend Raoul stops her.

"Forget that," he says, "come with me to Nuneaton. I'm about to take part in the running of the hamsters!"

Kirsty is incredulous. "Hamsters? That's not that scary!"

"Oh, but it is!" Raoul says. "There's about a thousand of them and they surge through the streets, gnashing their little teeth."

Kirsty is still unimpressed. "Yes, well, it still doesn't sound very scary."

"It is if you're dressed as a giant sunflower seed."

Where do hamsters go on their holidays?
Hamsterdam.

★ ★ ★ ★ ★ ★ ★ ★ ★ ★ ★

A man walks into a bar and says to a bartender, "If I show you a trick, will you give me a free drink?"

"Depends on how good a trick it is," the barman replies.

The man reaches into his pocket, pulls out a hamster and sits him behind the piano. The hamster starts to play the sweetest jazz riff the bartender has ever heard. He pours the man his drink. After finishing this, the man says, "If I show you another trick, can I have another free one?"

"If it is anything like that last one, you can drink free all night."

The man reaches into his other pocket, pulls out a rat, sits it on top of the piano, and the rat starts singing along with the hamster in a deep warm voice worthy of Frank Sinatra.

Impressed, the bartender starts to pour drinks as fast as the man can drink them.

After several hours, a big time Hollywood agent walks in, sees the act and frantically asks the bartender who it belongs to. The bartender points to the man, who's now a little worse for wear. The agent grabs him and says, "I will give you $1 million for that act."

"Not for sale," the man slurs.

"Right," the agent says, "how about $100,000 for just the singing rat?"

"You've got a deal!" the man says. The agent writes

him a cheque and leaves with the rat.

The bartender looks at the cheque and says, "Are you nuts? You had a million-dollar act that you just broke up for a hundred Gs?"

"Relax, pal," the man says. "The rat can't sing! The hamster's a ventriloquist."

* * * * * ★ ★ ★ * * * *

What's the difference between a hamster who has become a monk and a person cooking pork in a wok?
One is a hamster friar and the other is a ham stir-fryer.

★ ★

Why do hamsters stuff their cheeks?
Because if they stuffed their pockets their trousers would fall down.

• • • • • • • ● ● ● ● • • • •

Two hamsters in their cage.
"Shelagh, you're on that wheel day and night. Why?"
"I'm a revolutionary!"

• • • • • • ● ● ● ● ● • • • •

A girl attends a friend's party. She's let in the front door by her friend and welcomed with a hug. "Hey, glad you could come, it's through here, just throw your coat on the pile over there."

As she enters the front room, smooth music is playing and clusters of people are drinking and chatting. Over in the corner she notices a little hamster, who seems to be regaling a small crowd with a funny story.

"Uh, what's that?" the girl asks.

"Don't you know?" said her friend. "You can't have a party without Nibbles."

A hamster goes into a bar, sits down and orders a drink. The man on the stool next to him is amazed.

"You're a talking hamster!" he says.

"That's right. I've got a life and a job just like you," the hamster says.

"What's your job?"

"I'm a guinea pig"

"I thought you said you were a hamster."

"I am. But they do medical experiments on me."

Horses

Two racehorses are in their stables. One says to the other, "I was going down the back straight at Epsom, I was five lengths off the back of the pack, when suddenly I found this incredible energy from somewhere, came up the inside, and won by a nose."

"That's incredible," the other horse replies. "I was going full tilt over the sticks in the Grand National when over the last fence the jockey nearly fell off and ended up sitting on the top of my head. The only reason we won was that his bottom was first across the line!"

Then suddenly a voice from nowhere says, "Well, that's nothing."

They look down and see a greyhound. "I was running in the Greyhound Derby. Not only did I win the race, I caught the hare and ate it!"

The two horses turn to each other. "That's astonishing!" says one of the horses.

"I agree!" says his friend. "A talking greyhound?!"

A horse walks into a country inn. "Hey," says the barman. "Yes, please," says the horse.

In nineteenth-century England, Henry and Morris were walking home when they came across a man stuck in a ditch. They quickly helped him climb out, dusted him off and checked him for injuries. After establishing he was alright, the man patted them both on the back.

"Thanks so much, lads," he beamed. "I happen to run the largest stables in England and I promise that you shall each receive a new horse!"

Sure enough, the next day two horses were delivered to them. But it put them in a quandary. "How are we going to tell them apart?" asked Henry.

"I know, let's bob the tail of one of them, that'll do it."

They set to work but once they're finished they realise their mistake. "We've bobbed both the tails, that's no good. Okay, let's shave a triangle into the flank of one of them."

They do this, but once again realise they've put the triangle on both horses!

"Right, let's shave the mane off one of them," says Morris. And they do it, but lo and behold they've shaved both the manes off!

"Okay," says Henry. "You take the black one, I'll take the white one."

> A horse walks into a bar. The bartender says, "Why the long face?"
> And the horse says, "My wife left me."

★ ★

Every morning at 5 a.m. a man is woken by the sound of his wife coming back from her early morning horse ride: CLIP CLOP CLIP CLOP CLIP CLOP.

This goes on for months. Eventually he gets fed up and complains: "I can't stand it, clip clop clip clop, it drives me nuts! Can't you do something about it?"

She smiles. "I'll see what I can do."

The next morning he's woken up again at 5 a.m.: CLOP CLOP, CLIP CLIP, CLOP CLOP, CLIP CLIP.

His wife smiles in through the window: "I've taught him to moonwalk!"

★ ★

A man goes to his doctor and says his throat feels sore. The doctor shines a light into his mouth, and then nods. "Ah yes, you've got Shetland Pony."

"What do you mean?" asks the man.

"Well, you're a little hoarse."

A mounted policeman is engaged in a dramatic chase through the streets of the city in pursuit of El Ladrón, the world's greatest jewel thief. The felon had just completed his most daring raid ever – stealing the entire stock of Tiffany's – and was leaping and parkouring through the alleyways with abandon, the policeman and his steed in pursuit. Suddenly, the policeman's head is hit by a passing tree branch and in the second he takes his eyes off El Ladrón he is gone!

Back at headquarters the policeman is determined not to give up:

"It's true, I didn't see where he went... but my horse, Hercules, did!"

"That doesn't matter," says the commissioner. "There's no way to know the horse's mind!"

"I will find a way!" says the policeman.

He takes Hercules to a sophisticated lab, where the technicians probe, analyse and scan the horse. Using a series of tests and calculations and combining state-of-the-art brain-mapping technology with twenty-first century equestrian behavioural science and cutting-edge cryptography, they finally build a device capable of reading Hercules' mind. They put the helmet on the horse... nervously activate the power... and all peer at the screen:

oatsoatsoatsoat-
soatsoatsoatso-
atsoatsoatsoat-
soatsoatsoatso-
atsoatsoatsoats

In 1872, the former governor of California, Leland Stanford, a businessman and race-horse owner, hired English photographer Eadweard Muybridge for some photographic studies. He had taken a position on a popularly debated question of the day, whether all four feet of a horse were off the ground at the same time while galloping. To prove his case, Muybridge set out to capture this using the most sophisticated photographic techniques at the time.

What Muybridge found was amazing. Not only did the galloping horse have all four hooves off the ground but it also nipped off for a snack two minutes earlier and replaced itself with a well-trained gang of 14 dogs in a horse costume.

Two stablehands were working late one night when suddenly all of the lights in the stables went out at once. It was a pitch-black night, with no visible moon, and the darkness soon began to spook the horses. Eventually the stablehands discovered that the power cable had been chewed by rats. They tried to reattach it but with no success.

"I've got an idea!" said the taller of the stablehands. He split the wires down the middle and walked across the stable, attaching the wires to the horses heads one by one. Suddenly the lights sputtered back on. "See?" he said, "I just had to plug it into the manes."

Identity theft

A man is sitting somewhat dishevelled in a bar. His friend asks him what's wrong.

"What's wrong? I clicked on the wrong link in an email and they got into my system. They've cleared out my bank, they impersonated me at work, they've taken my house, my job, even my family! They've stolen my whole identity."

"Blimey, that's rough."

"Yeah, I wouldn't mind, but I've only had it three years myself!"

Two dodgy guys are sitting in an internet café. The first notices that the second has bandaged up hands.
"Oi, what happened to you?" he asks.

"Injured myself. I was getting the bank details off this old lady on the computer, and I was typing away furiously, but suddenly this other bloke is giving me his computer password, so I'm having to type to him too, then this couple are giving me their credit card number, so I'm typing like crazy..."

He holds up his hands.

"...and I got phishfingers."

A man on social media suddenly gets a message from his grandmother: "Help pls, am stuck in Spain with no passport or money, send me £500 via bank."

He writes back to her: "Hello, I'm not sure about this. You could be someone impersonating my gran, especially as I don't remember her saying she was going to Spain. Can you answer questions about my childhood?"

"Okay dear," she replies, "but hurry, please."

"Right," he begins, "what was my favourite childhood toy?"

"A teddy bear?"

"That's correct," he says. "What was its name?"

There is a pause before she says, "Ted?"

"Right again! But what colour was his little sweater?"

This time there is a longer pause: "Blue?"

"Blimey, Gran, you got them all right!"

"Yes dear," she says, "I've still got a good memory. Not bad for someone in my condition, eh?"

"You're telling me! You died two years ago!"

Insects

What do you call a fly
with no wings?
A walk.

A chap who lived on his own was feeling a bit lonely, so he went to the pet shop for something to keep him company. The pet shop owner suggested an unusual pet, a talking millipede.

"OK," thought the man, "I'll give it a go."

So he bought the millipede, took it back to his house and made it a temporary home in a cardboard box. That evening, testing his new pet, he leaned over the closed box and said, "I'm going to the pub for a drink, do you want to come too?" He waited a few moments, but there was no reply. He tried again, "Hey, millipede, wanna come to the boozer with me?" Again, no response. He decided to give it one more try before returning the millipede to the pet shop.

So he got very close to the box and repeated loudly, "I SAID I'M GOING TO THE PUB FOR A DRINK. DO YOU WANNA COME?"

"I heard you the first time," snapped the millipede. "I'm just putting my bloody shoes on!"

Inventions

Ben Franklin was flying a kite attached to a key in the middle of a thunderstorm when a passing villager stopped to speak to him.

"Look," said Ben Franklin, "I've made an amazing discovery!"

"Is it the kite? We've had those for years," the villager replied.

"No!" says Ben Franklin.

"Is it the key? Because we've got those too, for locking and unlocking doors."

"No, that's not it," says Ben Franklin.

"Is it nuclear fission?" asks the villager.

"Nuclear what?" says Ben Franklin.

"Oh nothing," says the villager. "I'm sure you'll get to that soon enough."

★ ★

Before the bulldog clip was invented, people would use real bulldogs. It was great for holding things together but made the paper really slobbery.

* * * * * ★ ★ ★ * * *

An inventor is trying to create the most effective mousetrap ever. He tries everything from pheromones to optical illusions to all kinds of foodstuffs, but nothing seems to work. Then he realises that what he really needs is an insight into the mouse's mind.

A colleague tells him, "Well, I've been experimenting with actual mice and we have one who can communicate with humans, so why don't you come and speak to him?"

The inventor is amazed and hurries off to the laboratory, where he is introduced to the mouse. He sits down next to it with a notepad.

"OK, so if you were creating a trap, what would you put in it?"

The mouse thinks about this carefully. "Alright, first it's got to be spacious. Not huge, but large enough to roam around in."

"Okay, great!" The inventor replies enthusiastically.

"And light. It's got to be well-lit and welcoming... a bit warm, too."

"Sure, that makes sense."

"And it should be soft inside, with places to sit."

"Right, I see."

"And there should be a TV, showing TED *Talks* and *Star Trek*."

"Really? Okay."

"...And maybe magazines scattered around, *New*

Scientist, Wired... and some attractive humans, sort of lounging about looking available. And every kind of computer game console."

The scientist stops writing and looks at the mouse. "Er... who is this a trap for, exactly?" He asks.

The mouse shrugged: "Well, I've been caught already, it must be your turn!"

★ ★ ★ ★ ★ ★ ★ ★ ★ ★ ★ ★ ★ ★

Two friends in a pub quiz team try to confer in a very noisy bar.

"Who invented the steam engine?"

"Watt?"

"I said, who invented the steam engine?"

"Watt!"

"I SAID, WHO INVENTED THE... Never mind. Who invented horsepower?"

"Watt?"

**Did you hear about this new invention, corduroy pillows!
They're making headlines.**

● ● ● ● ● ● ● ● ● ● ● ● ●

I wanted to put a joke here about inventing the wheel but I haven't got round to it yet.

● ● ● ● ● ● ● ● ● ● ● ● ●

An inventor has just finished a long period of development and confides in his friend, "I'm really worried about this new device I've created, it has some terrible side effects."

"Like what?"

"It causes your skin to turn red and peel off, boils erupt on your face, all your hair and teeth shrink and then fall out, you get wandering heart syndrome, your knees can explode and all your toes squidge together into one giant toe."

"Oh my, what does it do?"

"It lets you peel onions without crying."

"...I'll take three!"

★ ★

Everyone knows cavemen discovered fire by rubbing two flints together, but not many people know they also discovered water by rubbing hydrogen and oxygen together.

An inventor is trying to think of ways to make money. His friend advises him, "What you need to do is come up with something very simple that everyone in the world will need."

"Right!" he says, and sequesters himself in his lab for months. Eventually he emerges smiling, and shows his friend his creation. "I call it... the ladder!"

His friend looks at him incredulously. "But... the ladder already exists," he says.

"Ah, but this is The Ladder 2.0! You see... it only goes up! If someone uses it and wants to get down, they have to buy the special Down Ladder! That way we double our profits."

"I'm sorry, but that's ridiculous," his friend laughs. "Clearly they'll just buy the Up Ladder... and flip it over!"

John Logie Baird ran into the lab of one of his friends. "Och, I've finally cracked it!" he yelled. "Right now, out there, I've got a screen and I've managed to transmit to it – using the wireless signal – a series of white parallel horizontal lines!"

"Right," says his friend. "So what else is on?"

★ ★

The man who invented the vacuum cleaner had a lot of trouble getting his invention accepted. Whenever he tried to sell one, he would begin by telling people it sucked!

★ ★

Wernher von Braun, the famous rocket scientist, comes home late from a day of rocket science and finds his dinner cold, so he decides to prepare something for himself. He burns the toast... overcooks the beans... drops the eggs on the floor... and accidentally sets fire to the cat. His wife shakes her head: "Come on, Wernher, it's not that difficult. It's hardly brain surgery."

Two scientists talking at lunch.
"Did you hear about Watson? He's really been cut off at the knees!"
"What, did they pull his funding?"
"No, he was testing his spinning floor scythe."

At the turn of the nineteenth and twentieth century, the biggest problem facing scientists was that machinery which had been activated would keep going until it ran out of power or somehow malfunctioned. This was a cause of frustration for the inventors. Eventually one of them called a meeting to announce a new discovery.

"I have developed a new kind of 'switch' that when installed and activated, causes the devices to stop and enter a state of stasis! The purpose of this meeting is for you to assist me in devising a name for this wondrous appendage!"

The scientists began shouting out names.

"The automatic stoppinator."

"The no-go-anymore flange!"

"The non-animation deactivator!"

"The immediate cessation button!"

"The torpor-initiation toggle!"

After ten minutes of this, the scientist waved his arms frantically. "No, no, no! You know what? Let's just call it off."

Jokes

(A JOKE ABOUT JOKES)

It's the 1950s. A man is staying in a hotel in the Catskills after a business meeting nearby. He's not ready to go to bed yet, so he starts wandering around the place. Soon he finds himself in a large conference suite, coming into the back of the room where a row of chairs is occupied by around 200 people. At the front is a small stage. One by one, these men seem to be going up to the stage and reciting a single number... "73"... "145"... "231".... The other men laugh and nod with acknowledgement as they await their turn.

Confused, he turns to the man next to him: "Excuse me, I don't mean to intrude but what is this?"

The man smiles in a friendly way. "Oh, this is a stand-up comedians' convention! We're just having a little fun. You see, all the men here are such established joke-tellers that they know all the classic gags off by heart, so now all we have to do is go up and say the number of the joke in the official book and we all remember it!"

"Wow, that's amazing."

"Fancy having a go?" the man says, and leads the visitor to the front. He's nervous but approaches the stage. Leaning forward to the microphone, sheepishly he says, "Um... 876?"

The group collapses into fits of laughter, tears streaming down their cheeks. The man turns to his new friend, who's laughing just as hard. "Um... what just happened?" he asked.

"Oh, they'd never heard that one before!"

Journalists

A young reporter is desperate to speak with the United States Secretary of State. The problem is that he is well protected by his staff and bodyguards. He decides to try to talk to him during public appearances, like galas or fundraising dinners, but as soon as he gets close the Secretary immediately says, "I don't talk to journalists, you're all a bunch of liars and crooks!" And he's immediately ferried away by security staff.

He eventually figures out that the Secretary is a member of a particular country club. At great expense he signs himself up at the club under a false name. The Secretary is abroad, but the reporter goes to the country club for months to build up this false persona.

Eventually the Secretary returns to the country and begins going to the club again, and slowly the reporter gets closer to him, creating "accidental" meetings, occasional exchanged words, until he even manages to arrange for them to share a game of golf.

Even then, the reporter continues to play it cool. As further months pass, he gets closer and closer to the Secretary, until the man considers him to be a valued friend.

One day, as they both sit in a sauna together, the reporter decides the time is right. "Mr Secretary... Bob... can I ask you a question?"

The secretary turns to him with a warm, genuine smile: "Of course, Ryan, you can ask me absolutely anything."

The reporter hesitates, swallows, and then speaks: "...In one hundred words, what's your idea of a perfect Sunday?"

* * * * * ★ ★ ★ * * * *

A group of television reporters find themselves in a bar in a war-torn country.

"The situation here's terrible, but it's nothing like Angola," says one. "I was there for two months... the most horrifying thing I ever saw."

"I'm sure it was awful, but it can't compare to the three months I spent embedded during Vietnam," says another. "I still have nightmares."

"That's nothing," says a third. "When I was a cub reporter I had to cover a local birthday party."

"What?" says the first. "That's nothing like what we went through!"

"There were unlimited soft drinks and M&M's."

Their jaws collectively dropped with horror: "Oh my God, you poor man!"

A man is in the middle of what seems to be a successful job interview, when suddenly the interviewer fixes him with a piercing stare. "I have to reveal something," he says. "Your resumé claims that you went to Harvard University. We contacted them and they said they'd never heard of you. And down here you said that you'd interned at Goldman Sachs, but a phone call confirmed that wasn't true either. You never won a junior reporter award at your school, or made a viral vlog about local issues. In fact, your entire resumé is nothing but a tissue of lies!" The interviewer extends his hand. "Congratulations! You've got the job! You're going to fit in great here – let's get you a desk in the newsroom."

Kangaroos

A mummy kangaroo wakes up one morning and finds a koala in her pouch. "What are you doing here?" she asks.

"Well," the koala replies, "it was empty, it's nice and warm, and I can get about a bit quicker."

And the mummy kangaroo says, "Well, I'm sorry, but if you want to use it there's a waiting list – you'll have to book through Airbnb."

What do you get when you cross a kangaroo with a sheep? A woolly jumper!

Two kangaroos were sitting enjoying the afternoon sun. "So, what's the highest you think you've ever jumped?" asked the first.

"Well," the second kangaroo began, "I jumped seven feet once! I was hanging around by the lagoon, just having a drink, when I saw this thing that looked exactly like a log... but it turned out to be a crocodile! That thing was so fast, it started chasing me and I was hopping, but it was keeping up! So I came to this ravine and I figured it's now or never, and I took the biggest leap you can imagine – seven feet into the air – and landed the other side of the ravine! Such a lucky escape! So what about you? What's the highest you've ever jumped?"

"Oh, about 100 feet," came the reply.

The second kangaroo was amazed: "100 feet? What? Do you mean you jumped down into a deep hole."

"No, I jumped 100 feet vertically into the air."

"Really? But how?"

"Well, I'd been hopping all day and I was really tired. So I sat down on this log...."

What do you get when you cross a kangaroo with a horse?
Whinny the Roo.

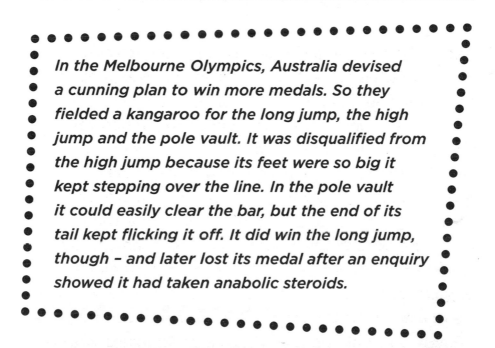

In the Melbourne Olympics, Australia devised a cunning plan to win more medals. So they fielded a kangaroo for the long jump, the high jump and the pole vault. It was disqualified from the high jump because its feet were so big it kept stepping over the line. In the pole vault it could easily clear the bar, but the end of its tail kept flicking it off. It did win the long jump, though – and later lost its medal after an enquiry showed it had taken anabolic steroids.

How does a kangaroo like its eggs?
Pouched.

What do you get when you cross a kangaroo with a hippo?
Hip hop!

Kangaroos are the only large mammals to use hopping for locomotion... except for Bill the Giant Mutant Bunny from Chernobyl.

★ ★

A joey said to its mother kangaroo, "Mum, it's time for me to grow up!"
"Oh, are you going to leave the pouch?"
"No, I just want people to start calling me Joseph."

What do you get when you put rollerskates on a kangaroo and give it a vacuum cleaner?
A kangaroomba!

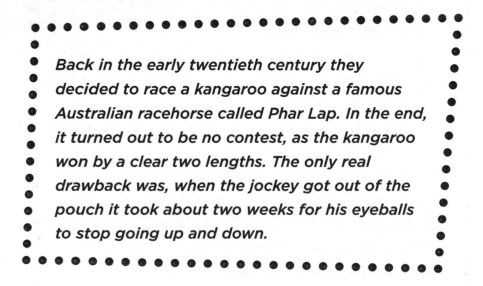

Back in the early twentieth century they decided to race a kangaroo against a famous Australian racehorse called Phar Lap. In the end, it turned out to be no contest, as the kangaroo won by a clear two lengths. The only real drawback was, when the jockey got out of the pouch it took about two weeks for his eyeballs to stop going up and down.

Knights

In his throne room King Callum is assigning duties to his assembled knights: "Sir Keen of Axe, you will go to the Mountains of Mopor, and there..."

King Callum is interrupted by sniggering coming from one of his Knights. He continues: "...there you will seek out Mighty Griddle..."

More snickering interrupts him: "...the black dragon, and slay him!"

Peals of laughter now ring out across the great hall. King Callum, now irritated, tries to carry on: "Sir Noble of Deeds..."

The laughter is now turning hysterical but the King soldiers on: "...Sir Noble of Deeds, you will go to the castle of..."

Hysterical, convulsive gasps of mirth continue. King Callum stops and suddenly roars: "WILL SOMEONE PLEASE REMOVE SIR FITZ OF GIGGLES FROM MY COURT!"

A damsel has been captured by a gang of evil bandits. She's tied up in the lair when suddenly in the doorway appears the noble Sir Gwedren. He leaps from his horse and immediately engages three bandits in a sword fight, cutting them down as they stand. He knocks down the biggest of them, then leaps off his back to swing from the chandelier and land on their hoard, scattering gold coins everywhere. He's inches from the damsel when suddenly he checks his watch, and immediately turns around and walks directly back to his horse, mounting it and beginning to ride away.

"Hey, wait!" shouts the damsel. "Where are you going?"

"Home," he says. "It's the end of my knight shift."

★ ★

One of the knights of Camelot begs an audience with King Arthur.

"What is it, Sir Bedevere?"

"Your Majesty, it's about the Round Table. You had it created for us because you said that as it has no head no one of us would be held above the others, and that even you, as our lord, would be equal to all of us despite our differing backgrounds."

"Yes, what of it?"

"Well, I don't think it's working."

"Why do you say that?"

"Because you tend to stand on it right in the middle, shouting: 'I'M THE KING! LOOK AT MY CROWN!'"

King Arthur is holding court over his men. "Sir Lancelot, you stand here accused of bringing shame upon your name and the court of Camelot with your unknightly conduct with Queen Guinevere. To restore your name, I task you with a series of quests.

First, you must go and defeat the Dragon of Cappadocia.

Then you must travel and defeat the Dragon of the Abyss.

Then you must find and kill the ancient Dragon of Mesopotamia.

And finally you must seek out and destroy the Dragon of Angarrack!"

Another knight puts his hand up: "Er, Your Majesty? Isn't that punishment a bit... dragonian?"

A lord calls one of his men before him. "Listen, Sir Beddings. I need you to go to my rival, Lord Colchester, and tell him he's an idiot. Then go to the landowners of Runnymede and tell them to soak their heads. Then you need to travel to Rome and be rude to the Pope."

The man splutters. "I couldn't possibly, sir, I am too kind of nature to be so hostile."

The lord sighs and nods. "Yes, of course, you're right... very well, bring me Sir Leigh."

A squire comes to a knight in his chambers, very apologetic.

"Sir, sir, I have some bad news. It's your armour, sir, it's rusted right through! There's not a single piece that isn't absolutely caked with rust."

"Is that correct, squire? Well, that's a dashed nuisance."

"What shall we do, sir?"

"Well, normally I would purchase some more, but my coffers have been somewhat light of late, so you shall have to scrape it all off."

"Really? But that will take many many hours, sir."

"Well, you'd better get started, then!"

So the squire goes off and dutifully begins scraping rust off every single piece of the armour: the helmet, the shoulders, the pauldrons, the gloves. After hours and hours of labour, he finally removes all of the rust and returns – exhausted – to his patron: "The armour is clear, sir."

"Excellent! Now help me put it on, it's time for my afternoon swim!"

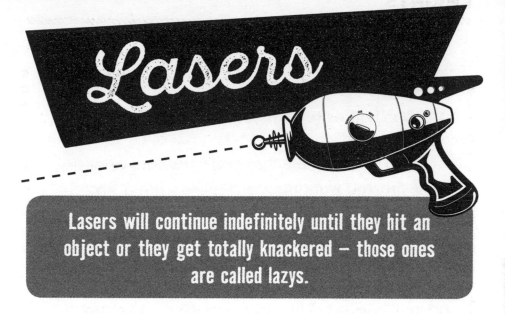

Lasers

Lasers will continue indefinitely until they hit an object or they get totally knackered — those ones are called lazys.

CDs and DVDs work by having their digitised contents read by a precision laser. But only during work time. In his spare time, the laser prefers to read the works of nineteenth-century dramatic novelist Victor Hugo.

●●●

Instead of lightbulbs, I've installed lasers all over my house. It's a lot faster and cheaper. The only problem I've had was the time the cat jumped on the dimmer switch. Still, I only have to buy one glove at a time now.

●●●

Two scientists decided to prove definitively, in laboratory conditions, that light travelled faster than sound. They would do this by firing a laser. The first scientist stood at one end of the room, and on the count of five, the second scientist fired the laser towards him. The second scientist then ran over to the first one excitedly. "We've proved it!" he shouted. "I definitely saw the laser hit you seconds before I heard you shout: 'OW, MY GROIN!'"

An inventor starts dragging a huge crate across his laboratory floor. The man who shares his workspace watches for a bit, then, resigned, goes over to help him. "Thanks so much," the exhausted inventor says.

"What are you working on?" says the other inventor, curious.

"Oh, I've developed an amazing new method for making toast from agar. You fire a specially focused laser and you can zap any piece of bread from a distance of up to a mile in a millisecond. It's brilliant."

The second inventor looks baffled. "So it's a really big laser, is it?"

The first inventor shakes his head. "No, it's incredibly lightweight and you can fit it in your pocket."

The second inventor points to the crate. "So what's this, then?"

"Oh, that's the trebuchet that you use to put the marmalade on."

* * * * * ★ ★ ★ * * * *

Many people accidentally spell it "lazer" instead of "laser". What they don't realise is that LASER stands for LIGHT AMPLIFICATION BY STIMULATED EMISSION OF RADIATION... whereas LAZER stands for LET'S ALL ZAP EACH OTHER'S REAR-ENDS!

* * * * * ★ ★ ★ * * * *

An army chief is in his office planning the next assault when his lieutenant walks in.

"Sir, we have a problem with these new laser guns you've given us."

"What's the problem, son?"

"Well, we've been testing them on night missions and the problem is you can't see who you're firing at until you've already fired the gun."

"Ah, right. Well, why don't you fire a warning shot to the side, and then you can illuminate the people so you can hit them?"

"We've tried that, but obviously as soon as you fire a warning shot they know where you are and they duck out of the way."

"Hmm, yes. Okay, why don't you fire a warning shot behind you. That'll give you enough ambient light to see them, won't it?"

"We tried that too, sir, but if you do that you risk hitting one of your fellow troops standing behind you."

"Yes, I can see that." The army chief ponders the problem. "I've got it. Fire a warning shot directly up into the sky. Then you will be able to see your combatant easily."

"Alright," the lieutenant agrees, "we'll try that, sir." And he heads out of the office.

Ten minutes later, a battered and bleeding air pilot wearing a smouldering flightsuit and carrying a mangled helmet walks in: "Sir, we've got a different problem."

Two scientists decided to see what would happen if they fired their lasers directly at each other. Their funerals are next Thursday. (You'll need to crowd around because the coffins are very small.)

An ambitious entertainments manager commissions the building of the biggest club ever in his home city. To match this, he also decides to commission the building of the world's biggest disco ball. Seventy feet in diameter, utilising more panels of mirrored glass than the Doge's Palace in Venice, the ball is hauled to the ceiling by six hydraulic power-winches. Activated, the beams of light flying across the dance floor are totally dazzling.

Two hours into their first night, the floor manager runs into his office, sweating. "The disco ball is too strong! The light is being converted into sweeping giant lasers that are spinning round the room and blasting people directly in the face. We've had to evacuate! We'll be sued to ribbons!"

The manager thinks about this very carefully. "Alright, I know exactly what to do." He makes his way down to the lobby, bypassing the disco ball room, and then to the front of the club. Very carefully he writes a sign and pins it to the door: "FREE LASER EYE SURGERY WITH EVERY TICKET PURCHASED."

Professor Jenkins was talking enthusiastically to her boyfriend. "Guess what, I decided to do something really romantic. So I wrote your name on the moon with a laser!"

Her boyfriend was shocked. "Uh, I love you honey, but that's terrible, an eyesore – you've ruined the moon forever."

Professor Jenkins rolled her eyes. "Don't worry, I used that moon probe we sent to reflect the laser back, and I wrote your name on the dark side so it can't be seen."

The boyfriend looks relieved. Then he sees the clouds drift away from the moon, and sees etched directly on its surface: "P.T.O."

★ ★

Two robots are in their recharge bays having a conversation.

"You know, it's amazing," says one. "Two years ago I was in a car manufacturing plant, making SUVs on an assembly line. Now I've been completely repurposed. I spent all yesterday in an operating theatre, performing keyhole surgery with a precision medical laser."

"Wow!" says the second robot. "So did it go well?"

"Well, the heart bypass went great... but they got a bit upset when I installed the wing mirrors and gear stick."

Lotteries

Sheila, Barbara and Jessie were talking about playing the lottery. "I've got a system!" said Sheila. My lottery numbers are my birthday plus my daughter's birthday.

"I've got a system too!" said Barbara. "My numbers are the player numbers of my six favourite footballers. Foolproof!"

"That's very good," said Jessie. "My numbers are 1, 2, 3, 4, 5 and 6."

"Well, there's no chance of those ever coming up!" said Sheila incredulously.

"Actually," said Jessie, "statistically there's as much of a chance of that coming up as any other combination."

Her friends were skeptical, but that Saturday the lottery numbers were announced, and they were 1, 2, 3, 4, 5 and 6! They were amazed. Barbara phoned Jessie.

"Oh my God, you were right!" Barbara exclaimed.

"I know!" said Jessie. "Now, where do I buy a ticket?"

The group in charge of generating the lottery numbers were putting the numbered balls into the machine when suddenly an electrical failure caused it to short circuit, sending thick black smoke up into the air. After an extensive check, they realised the machine was totally dead.

"What are we going to do! We have to announce the numbers in an hour!" said one of the crew members, panicking. "We need to come up with a new way of randomly generating the numbers."

After a few unsuccessful suggestions, one man stepped forward.

"Give me the balls. I learned how to juggle last year, I'll toss them in the air."

"All forty?" asked the crew member incredulously.

"Sure!" said the man, "and then the first six I drop can be the numbers!"

With no better idea available, they shrugged and passed him the balls. Twenty minutes later, the man was still juggling them! The crew member hissed at him incredulously, "You're juggling forty balls, how is it possible that you haven't dropped a single one yet?"

"I've no idea," he says, "but call the Guinness Book of Records*!"*

Three mates were speculating about how they'd spend their money if they won millions in the lottery.

"I'd get myself a yacht... not a little one, but one of those super-yachts. They're basically just floating luxury apartments!" said one. "Full staff, all mod cons, just pure luxury helm to stern."

"Well," said the second, "I'd buy my local footie team, you know, Rundown Park Rangers. Pour my money into their coffers, let them buy a new stadium, all the best players, steam on up to the Premier League!"

"Nice!" says the third friend. "I'd buy myself some teabags."

"Just teabags?" said the first man, incredulously.

The third man slaps his forehead.

"Oh, you're right, I'm being stupid. I'm going to be a multi-millionaire!... I'll buy some biscuits too."

★ ★

A man receives an email declaring that he's won $30 million in MESO, the Mesopotamian lottery! He can't believe his luck and tells his friend excitedly.

"Nah, that's not real," says his friend, "it's spam."

"Don't be ridiculous," says the man. "SPAM is the Danish lottery!"

A group of lottery winners decide to form a club, to allow them to share stories of their new wealth and collaborate with investments. At one of the meetings some new members had joined and were asked how much they had won.

"I got £3 million," said the first. "After tax."

"I've been blessed with just under £15 million, gentlemen!" said the second man, beaming.

"I got three numbers and won a tenner," said the third.

Everyone looked at him with distaste. "You know this is supposed to be a club for people who won millions, don't you?" asked the first man.

"Oh yeah!" said the third. "I was hoping I could borrow some."

Two women were buying their lottery tickets when a friend passed by and scoffed at them: "What a waste of money. Only total idiots buy lottery tickets."

They gave her a dirty look but otherwise said nothing. The next week they saw her driving up in a very expensive convertible car. "Hey, guess what," she shouted, leaning out of the car. "I won the lottery!"

The women were incensed. "But I thought you said only total idiots buy lottery tickets."

"I know," said their friend. "I got it by accident... I thought I was buying a sandwich."

A man who regularly played scratch cards would occasionally win a prize of £10, which he would immediately use to buy more scratch cards. One day he scratched off the silver and let out a cry of amazement. "Wow... it says here I've won £500,000!"

Smiling, he handed the card to the shopkeeper: "Give me 500,000 pounds' worth of scratchcards please."

The shopkeeper looked at him with horror: "No, no sir, you can't do that! I mean, I don't even have that amount of scratchcards! But you must use it for something else, you know... travel the world!" The man thought about this and nodded.

A week later, he came back in the shop smiling. "So, did you travel the world?" The shopkeeper asked him.

"Oh yeah! I mean, I had to, otherwise how could I visit enough shops to sell me 500,000 pounds' worth of scratchcards?"

Why should you never iron a four-leaf clover?
You should never press your luck!

A woman is setting up a community garden and wonders if she can get some funding for it from the National Lottery. She downloads the necessary application forms and fills in sheaves of paper with personal details, information about the garden and her plans for it, and even personal information about the people who are going to help her. Then she has to attend a series of meetings and assessments, as well as five or six inspections of the proposed site.

After about six months she receives word that she has been approved for lottery funding! The following day an official comes to her house, and with great formality... hands her a lottery ticket.

"Is that it?" she asks incredulously.

"Of course not!" he says, and hands her a note that reads: "GOOD LUCK".

A general noticed one of his soldiers behaving oddly. The soldier would pick up any piece of paper he found, frown and say: "That's not it" and put it down again. This went on for some time, until the general arranged to have the soldier psychologically tested. The psychologist concluded that the soldier was deranged, and wrote out his discharge from the army. The soldier picked it up, smiled and said: "That's it!"

★ ★

Money

A young man goes to his father and asks to borrow a large sum of money. His dad decides a lecture would be more suitable. "Listen, son," he says. "Money can't buy you happiness, or stability, or love, or a better future."

"That's all true, Dad," the son says, "but it can buy me a Lamborghini Aventador."

> **People say money is the root of all evil. Personally, I think it's turnips. They're disgusting!**

A frog goes into a bank and walks up to the teller, whose name is Pat Wack. "Good Morning, Miss Wack," he says. "My name is Kermit Jagger and I want to take out a loan for £10,000."

She looks at him curiously. "Do you have any collateral?"

He holds up a pink china elephant: "This is it."

"Just a moment, please," she says, "I'll have to go and see the manager." She goes into the manager's office and says, "There's a frog outside whose name is Kermit Jagger – he wants a loan of £10,000 and all he can raise as collateral is a pink china elephant.

Surprised, he looks at her and replies: "Nicknack Patty Wack? Give the frog a loan. His old man's a Rolling Stone!"

A woman asks another woman if she has a coin. The second woman scoffs at this: "Coin? We live in a cashless society now. From swipeable debit cards to online payment methods and even entirely virtual currencies, the ephemeral nature of our monetary system in the twenty-first century has rendered physical money redundant!"

The first woman says, "Look, ref, we're not going to be able to start this game until we've done the coin toss."

A wealthy old man is walking along the street when a knife-wielding mugger jumps out of the shadows. "Gimme yer wallet and that fancy watch!" he says.

"Ah, well, you see," says the wealthy man, "you can take these material goods, but pretty soon the money will be gone and you'll be back with nothing again. These were earned with graft and honest hard work, and with a decent appreciation of the importance of squeezing every penny..."

"Listen..." the mugger tries to interrupt, but the man continues.

"...and it's only through understanding the true value of these things..."

"Ugh, I give up!" Exasperated, the mugger throws down his knife.

"And that's the other problem," the man continues. "Young people nowadays give up so easily."

A film director makes a worried conference call to his producer.

"The movie's solid but it's really uninspiring, actually kind of dull. It's a real problem."

"Well, we've got a bit of leeway on the budget," the producer replies. "We're transferring £10 million to you. Throw some money at the production."

The director agrees. Two weeks later he contacts them again, even more upset. "It's even worse than before!" he tells them.

"Really? Did you throw some money at it?"

"I certainly did, and the actors all quit – they were sick of getting hit by coins!"

In the 1920s, a broke university student decides to hit up his wealthy father for some cash and heads to the telegraph office. When he gets there, he realises the telegram charges by the letter and he doesn't have enough money for a long message. Thinking hard, he eventually sends one saying:

"No Mon. Stop. No Fun. Stop. Your Son."

After a few days of hand-wringing, he receives a message back.

"I'm Sad. Stop. Too Bad. Stop. Your Dad."

Monks

A monastery falls on hard times, so two monks decide to start a fish and chip shop. On the first day of opening, a woman comes in and sees one of the monks peeling spuds. "You must be the chipmonk!" she says to him. "No," he replies, "I'm the friar."

A man finds out about a monastery located high in the hills. The only way to get to it is to take a thirty-minute ride in a basket, being hoisted up the cliff face. The man decides this would be an adventurous thing to do, so he asks the monk at the bottom of the cliff whether he can get a lift up. The monk agrees and they begin the journey. About halfway up, the man notices that the rope pulling the basket is very frayed. Slightly worried, he asks the monk, "How often does this rope get replaced?"

The monk thinks on this for a few seconds and replies, "Whenever it breaks."

Movies

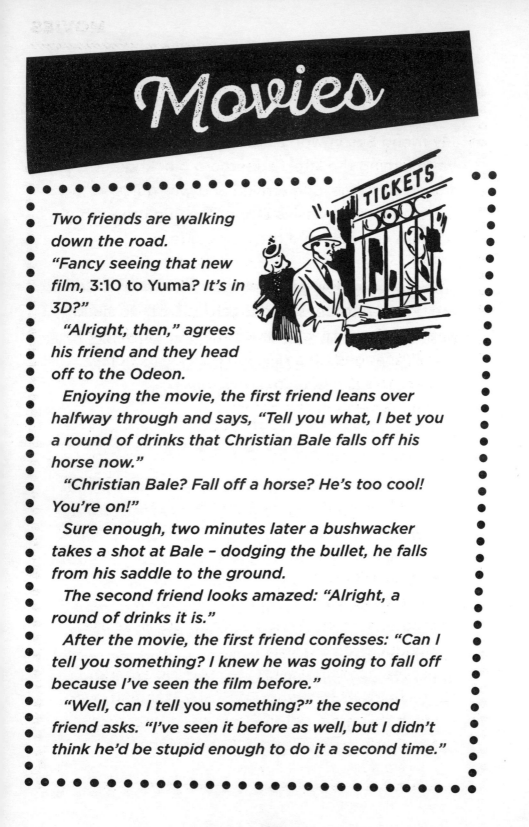

Two friends are walking down the road.
"Fancy seeing that new film, 3:10 to Yuma? It's in 3D?"

"Alright, then," agrees his friend and they head off to the Odeon.

Enjoying the movie, the first friend leans over halfway through and says, "Tell you what, I bet you a round of drinks that Christian Bale falls off his horse now."

"Christian Bale? Fall off a horse? He's too cool! You're on!"

Sure enough, two minutes later a bushwacker takes a shot at Bale – dodging the bullet, he falls from his saddle to the ground.

The second friend looks amazed: "Alright, a round of drinks it is."

After the movie, the first friend confesses: "Can I tell you something? I knew he was going to fall off because I've seen the film before."

"Well, can I tell you something?" the second friend asks. "I've seen it before as well, but I didn't think he'd be stupid enough to do it a second time."

My friend Susan won a studio tour, where they were filming the latest superhero blockbuster franchise movie. She arrived and was quickly ushered into a massive empty-looking green room.

'There you go," said the tour guide.

"But... where's the set?" she asked.

"Oh, it's all computer-generated nowadays. Sets are deemed to be very dangerous, both to build and to be on. You could get knocked down by a wall, snagged on a nail, run over by a cherry picker... this is much cheaper."

"But... where are the actors?"

"The actors earn so much money now they can't even go near a studio, they're all insured for millions of dollars and the insurance company won't let them out of their homes! They all perform in special padded rooms in their villas."

"But... shouldn't there be technicians?" she asked, bewildered.

"No, they're all at home in front of their computer screens. The only risk there is a stale doughnut or a cold latte!"

"Let me get this straight. No set? No actors? No technicians? So who's that guy standing over there in the middle of the floor? The director?"

"No, that's the Health and Safety inspector."

Two colleagues are leaving the office.

"What are you doing tonight, Tracy?" asks Matt.

"Oh, we're going to watch *Texas Chainsaw Massacre* on Netflix."

"Oh, is someone looking after your kids?"

"No, they're going to be there."

"Seriously? What about all the violence?"

"I've devised a foolproof way that we can watch any film with our kids, no matter how violent! Anytime something really nasty happens onscreen, I jump up in front of it and sing nursery rhymes!"

"And that works?"

"Mostly, but I started with 'Oranges and Lemons', and I got to the bit where there's a chopper chopping off their heads..."

"What happened then?"

"My wife jumped up in front of me and started singing 'Three Blind Mice'."

Two old ladies are having brunch together.

"Ooh, I tell you," says the first, "I got up at 5 a.m. this morning and immediately went off down the road, holding a house brick in each hand!"

"Blimey!" says the second old lady. "On your mobility scooter?"

"That's right!" she replied. "Then I went to the butchers. He was surprised to see me. I went into the freezer and hammered seven bells out of a side of frozen beef with my handbag!"

"Then what?" asks the second lady.

"Then, I made my way to the town hall and went up and down the stone entrance steps at least ten times with my zimmer frame! And once I was at the top I punched the air dramatically in triumph!"

"Well," says the second old lady, "it sounds like you had a bit of a Rocky start."

What's ET short for?
Because he's got little legs.

A businessman is talking excitedly to one of his friends. "Guess what? I'm in charge of the next Secret Cinema production! It'll be epic. We've built a one-to-one scale model of the *Titanic*! Everyone gets on board and we sail across the Atlantic while they watch the movie, surrounded by people dressed in the style of the time – crew, passengers, DiCaprio and Winslet lookalikes. And – here's the kicker – when the ship hits the iceberg on the screen we'll ram the actual ship into a replica iceberg! It's made of real ice, specially towed in from the Antarctic!"

His friend looks horrified. "You can't do that! Thousands of people will die! It's incredibly dangerous!"

The businessman looks uncertain. "Really? Okay, hang on a tick." He picks up his phone and makes a call. "Hello, George? I think we'd better call back *The Hindenberg Experience*!"

★ ★

A film director a scriptwriter, and a producer are walking along a road when they find an antique oil lamp. They rub it and a genie comes out in a puff of smoke.

"I usually only grant three wishes," the genie says, "so I'll give each of you just one."

"Me first! Me first!" says the film director. "I wish I was on a desert island, just clean food and water and beautiful calm." Whoosh! He's gone.

The scriptwriter says, "I want to be with my family, all together having dinner just like it always used to be." Whoosh! He's gone.

The producer looks at the genie... and says, "Get those idiots back here!"

A while back, a group of Hollywood producers decided to make a film of the life of Joan of Arc. They approached Steven Spielberg and asked if he were interested. "You bet!" he said. "The way I see it, Joan goes on a magical quest to get the holy grail, she ends up in the jungle being chased by a giant stone ball, eventually she reconciles with her dad, and then aliens..."

"Stop, stop there, Mr Spielberg!" they said.

Next they asked Martin Scorsese if he were interested. "Oh sure! The way I see it, Joan is a backstreet kid with attitude, she gets in with the wrong crowd, she's snortin' cocaine off a giant shield, then she mows down a bunch of knights with a machine gun, uh, crossbow, then..."

"Thanks, but no thanks, Mr Scorsese," they said.

Finally, they approached the great auteur Stanley Kubrick. Would he do it?

"I think so," he said. "I'll go to every historical archive to find the real Joan – maybe the Vatican will even unseal some documents. I'll craft an authentic, respectful biopic of a woman revered throughout Christendom."

The producers sighed with relief. "That's fantastic, Stanley. The job's yours."

"Thank you," he replied. "See you in twenty years."

★ ★

I was going to the cinema and my mate Dennis asked what I was going to see. *"Moby Dick!"* I said.

"Oh, what's that about, then?" he asked.

"Whales. Wanna come?"

"No thanks, I can't stand Welsh people."

★ ★

Museums

Some tourists in the Chicago Museum of Natural History were marvelling at the dinosaur bones. One of them asked the guard, "Can you tell me how old the dinosaur bones are?"

"They are three million, four years, and six months old," the guard replied.

"That's an awfully exact number," says the tourist. "How do you know their age so precisely?"

"Well," the guard answered, "the dinosaur bones were three million years old when I started working here, and that was four-and-a-half years ago."

Music

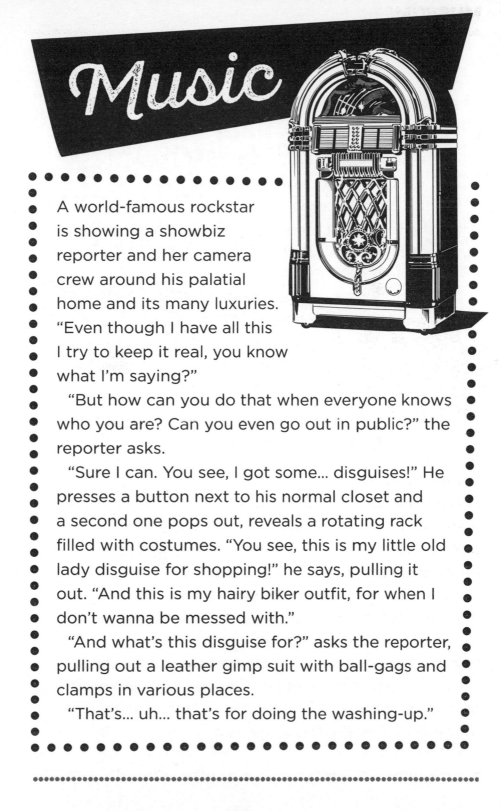

A world-famous rockstar is showing a showbiz reporter and her camera crew around his palatial home and its many luxuries. "Even though I have all this I try to keep it real, you know what I'm saying?"

"But how can you do that when everyone knows who you are? Can you even go out in public?" the reporter asks.

"Sure I can. You see, I got some... disguises!" He presses a button next to his normal closet and a second one pops out, reveals a rotating rack filled with costumes. "You see, this is my little old lady disguise for shopping!" he says, pulling it out. "And this is my hairy biker outfit, for when I don't wanna be messed with."

"And what's this disguise for?" asks the reporter, pulling out a leather gimp suit with ball-gags and clamps in various places.

"That's... uh... that's for doing the washing-up."

Two crusty old rockers are sitting around reminiscing about their pasts.

"Hey, Sticks, remember that gig up in that ruined castle in Scotland?"

"I sure do," says Sticks. "Rained so hard we couldn't see our own hands, let alone the soggy audience."

"And what about that gig in that ratty old bar in Akron? When that fire started?"

"Sure I remember," says Sticks, "I started the fire – I didn't want to do an encore."

"You wild man! And remember that gig in that awful field in Cornwall."

Sticks shakes his long hair. "Nope. Don't remember it."

"You don't?!"

"No, man. I've only got a two gig memory."

A band are just setting up for a gig at a concert hall. One of the technicians goes up to the lead guitarist. "So, uh, how long are you boys planning to play for?"

"We don't know. You see, our lead singer has narcolepsy. He could literally fall asleep at any time. So we just play until that happens. It might be two hours, it might be two minutes, no real clue."

"But what about all these people who have paid money to see you play? Shouldn't you just try to carry on? Or get a new lead singer?"

"We would, but he's the one who drives the tour bus!"

A man agreed to buy bass guitar lessons for his son.

At the end of the first week, the man asked his son what he had learned and the son said, "For my first lesson, I learned all about the E string."

The man was quite pleased and told him to carry on. At the end of the second week, he asked his son what he had learned that week. The son replied, "This week, I learned all about the A string."

His father nodded but seemed a bit worried about how slowly the lessons were progressing.

At the end of the third week, he said to his son, "You know, these lessons cost a fair amount. What did you learn this week?"

"Oh," said the son. "No problem. I quit the lessons. I already got a gig."

A manager is having a meeting with his pop band about promoting their upcoming album. "OK, we're going to need a video for your first single. Now, in this modern era every band has these videos where they do weird stunts or optical illusions or whatever... like those guys who were on the treadmills, or that band who sang while sky-diving. So I've hired the world's biggest food blender! You'll all sit on the edge of it singing and playing, the blades will start up, and as the song goes on, one by one you'll plunge into it, and turn instantly into a sort of human milkshake."

The band nod enthusiastically, impressed. "And it'll be done with CGI, right?" one asks.

"Nope."

"So, it'll be practical effects, like dummies or something."

"Nope, no faking. You're going to go in there for real!"

The band look at each other concerned. "But if we do that, we'll be... dead!"

"Well," the manager shrugs, "you ain't getting a deal on a second album, so really, who gives a frig?"

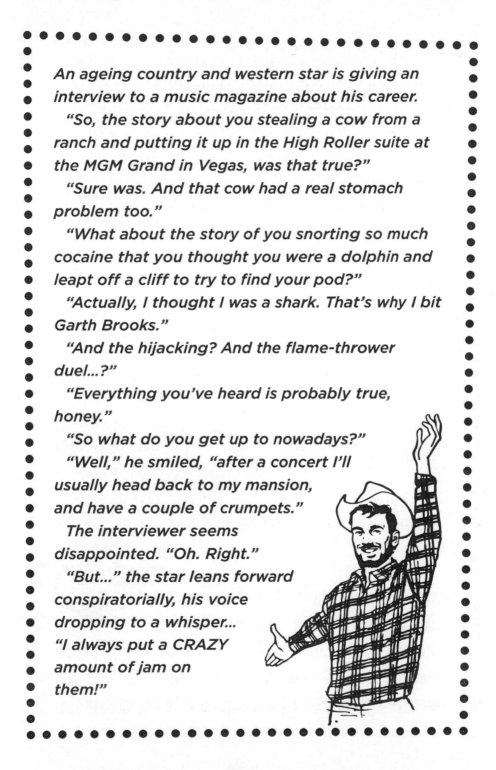

An ageing country and western star is giving an interview to a music magazine about his career.

"So, the story about you stealing a cow from a ranch and putting it up in the High Roller suite at the MGM Grand in Vegas, was that true?"

"Sure was. And that cow had a real stomach problem too."

"What about the story of you snorting so much cocaine that you thought you were a dolphin and leapt off a cliff to try to find your pod?"

"Actually, I thought I was a shark. That's why I bit Garth Brooks."

"And the hijacking? And the flame-thrower duel...?"

"Everything you've heard is probably true, honey."

"So what do you get up to nowadays?"

"Well," he smiled, "after a concert I'll usually head back to my mansion, and have a couple of crumpets."

The interviewer seems disappointed. "Oh. Right."

"But..." the star leans forward conspiratorially, his voice dropping to a whisper... "I always put a CRAZY amount of jam on them!"

A huge international orchestra is rehearsing for their upcoming concert at Carnegie Hall. They're playing absolutely beautifully – from the woodwind to the brass they are all at the top of their game. The only problem is that at a certain point, the timpani drummer keeps coming in on the wrong bar.

Eventually the conductor takes him aside. "What's going on, you keep coming in slow. Have you got your sheet music?"

"Yes, I do maestro."

"And you can see me with the baton?"

"I can, I can!"

"Then you must try to get it right. This is the finale, the *1812 Overture*!"

"Is it? Oh, sorry, my watch is a minute slow, I thought it was 1811!"

Ninjas

My best friend told me I was obsessed with ninjas and ninja weaponry. When I disputed this he said, "You are, constantly talking about nunchaka and bo staffs! I bet you can't say a single sentence that doesn't have anything to do with ninja." And I replied, "Shuriken!"

Two guards were standing on a rooftop, armed with sniper rifles, defending a military compound. All around was darkness, when suddenly they heard the sound of something metallic being dropped, and a whispered "Oops!" Then they heard a wooden staff being dropped and someone else yelling out: "Ow! My foot, you idiot!" They heard nothing else... Then suddenly out of the darkness three black-clad figures leapt acrobatically... before slipping on the roof tiles and falling to their deaths.

"Just as I thought," said one of the guards, "butterninjas."

> How many ninjas does it take to change a lightbu... oh wait, it's already been changed.

* * * * ★ ★ ★ ★ * * *

A man decides to join a group of ninjas. After years of training and searching, he is finally permitted access to a secret dojo high up in the mountains. He becomes an initiate and after further years of training establishes himself as one of the best warriors in the group – surpassing even those who had been there from birth. His trainer is proud to call him his finest warrior.

"Tomorrow you will be sent on your first true mission," the master says, giving the man his jet-black true ninja outfit for the first time. On the master's prompting he puts it on, but he looks very unhappy.

"Master," the man says, "I have something to

confess. You see, on her deathbed my mother made me promise only to wear bright neon pink."

"Ah, I see," says the master. "That explains your wardrobe while you trained here. We just assumed you were strapped for cash."

"Oh no, it was a promise," the man says. "The problem is when I go out on my mission I'm going to have to wear a neon-pink ninja outfit and I worry that it will make me totally visible."

"I see," said the master, frustrated, but unwilling to question a pact that the young man made out of respect for his elder. "I have a solution. We will take the pink outfit and we will dip it in hot tar. That way it will still be pink underneath, it will just be very dirty. And therefore you will not be seen."

A day later the master receives news that the young man had been killed. "NO!" says the ninja master. "But did he not dip his ninja outfit in hot tar, as I asked?"

"He did, master," replied the messenger. "But maybe he should have taken it off first."

* * * * * ★ ★ ★ * * * *

The group of ninjas arrived outside the office complex swathed in total darkness.

The master of the group turned to the youngest, the initiate. "Ordinarily," he said, "I would send in my most experienced pupil, but the vents of this building permit only people of small stature to enter, so this has become your moment of reckoning."

"Yes, master."

"And on another day I would expect you to improvise and rely on your training to locate the target, but he must be assassinated tonight, or we will miss our chance for many years."

"Yes, master."

"For this reason I will give you precise instructions and you must follow them very carefully. To the letter."

The master proceeded to outline a step-by-step plan to bypass the guards, eliminate the security cameras, leap through the laser projections, and then perform an elaborate double-backing through the entire building to ensure his trail couldn't be followed. "You will then find yourself in his central office, and the target will be sitting behind his desk."

The initiate nodded, and immediately leapt into the darkness. Two hours later he returned, bruised and scarred, but grinning.

The master questioned him: "You followed the instructions."

"Yes, master."

"You avoided the guards? Destroyed the cameras? Dodged the lasers? Went through the whole office? Found him in his lair?"

"Yes, master."

The master now grinned himself. "So, finally our arch-nemesis is dead, slain by your hand!"

The initiate suddenly looked sheepish. "Um... was that in the instructions, master?"

* * * * * ★ ★ ★ ★ * * * *

* * * * * ★ ★ ★ ★ * * *

A young man named Dave had just moved to a small town. He found it to be pretty normal, with everyone there friendly, if a little wary of strangers – about how you'd imagine small-towners to be. One day, Dave was walking down to the main high street when he heard a great hubbub of people talking, and noticed a huge crowd assembling in the town square. And every single person was dressed entirely in black, wearing ninja masks. He was baffled. Recognising the distinctive glasses of his neighbour Ted, he sidled up to him and asked him what was happening.

"It's the Ninja Festival," said Ted with a smile. "This time every year we dress up as ninjas and perform ninja activities. It was started by the town founders. They were also ninjas, you see."

Dave was puzzled but smiled too. "Ninja festival, huh? Can I get a costume too?"

Ted scratched his head. "Ah, well, you see, that's the thing Dave. The person who's the latest to move into town becomes the... uh... kind of the target. They get twenty minutes to hide and then we hunt them across the town using our skills of stealth and acrobatics. Afterwards we display the corpse in the town hall during the annual ninja buffet."

Dave laughed... but quickly realised from the expression on his face that Ted was deadly serious. Suddenly aware of being surrounded by people dressed in black clothing and armed with shiny weaponry, Dave knew he had to run for his life. Suddenly he stopped himself. "Hey, wait a minute!" he said. "I wasn't the last person to move into town! Gina Fulton is – she moved in last week!"

"That's true, Dave, but the thing is... she makes these amazing oatmeal cookies."

* * * * * ★ ★ ★ ★ ★ * * *

A man noticed a shop in his area called Ninja Dry Cleaners. He went inside to find what seemed to be a pretty typical dry cleaning establishment.

"Why are you called Ninja Dry Cleaners?" he asked. "Do you get things clean really fast?"

"Nope," said the bored looking woman behind the counter. "Pretty much the usual speed."

"Okay, so do you do an amazing job, like strike at the heart of stains and make them disappear as if they were never there?"

"Not really," said the woman. "To be honest we do a pretty crappy job."

"Really? So... do you only dry clean black clothing?"

"Nope, we do anything."

"Do you only work at night?"

"Nah, we close at 6 p.m."

The man was exasperated. "So, why are you called Ninja Dry Cleaners?"

"Hang on, I'll call for the manager. MR NINJA! A CUSTOMER HAS A QUESTION!"

Nuclear

A man is proudly showing his neighbour around his newly completed nuclear bunker. "This baby has everything!" he boasts. "Down there we have bedrooms, a kitchen, communal areas, even a simulated garden. I've got a water filtration unit that'll be good for 75 years, enough canned food for the same time, a hydroponic garden so I've got clean air. And the whole thing is sealed in titanium. The door seal closes so quickly, all I need to do is be here five minutes before a nuclear attack and we'll all be safe. So, what do you have?"

The neighbour blinks. "I got a shotgun."

The man smirks. "Well, that's nice, Paul, but I don't think a shotgun's going to save you from the blast."

"It will if I get here five minutes before a nuclear attack as well!"

> Woman to her boyfriend: "Your brain is so small, if you ever had a split personality it would cause an atomic explosion."

A nuclear scientist returns to her lab in the morning, ready for another day of vital work. She comes just in time to see the cleaner leaving, and gives him a friendly wave. Suddenly, she notices with horror that the cleaner has wiped off the huge blackboard occupying the entire back wall!

"What have you done?!" she shouts, pointing at the blackboard.

"Oh yeah, I had to wipe it... it was covered in scribbles..."

She grabs his shoulders. "You fool! That was hours, perhaps days of calculations, vital to my work and even our national interest!"

The cleaner pulls himself free. "OK, hold on. It so happens that I have a photographic memory, and I saw the whole thing."

The scientist is sceptical. "Really?"

"Sure. Gimme a piece of chalk."

Sure enough, the cleaner begins writing everything back onto the board as it was before, right down to the exact digits and symbols. When he's 90 per cent done, he suddenly stops. The scientist's eyes widen. "What? Have you forgotten it? Oh my God! The project is doomed, we don't have time..."

He turns to look at her: "No, I ran out of chalk."

///

The year is 2219. A homeowner is showing his new robot butler around the house for which it'll be responsible.

"Okay, in the kitchen here we have the super-fast oven, that's nuclear powered. And the toaster, that's nuclear-powered too. And over here there's the waste bin, that's nuclear-powered.

"Sir, might I ask something?" says the butler.

"Yes, Chippington?"

"Is it fair to assume that everything in this house is nuclear-powered?"

The homeowner thinks about this. "Um... the bed is... the TV... the drapes... yes, it's all nuclear-powered."

"Sir... am I nuclear-powered?" the robot asks.

"Oh no, Chippington. You're powered by clockwork."

The butler is taken aback. "Really, sir?"

"No!" laughs the man. "I was just winding you up!"

★ ★ ★ ★ ★ ★ ★ ★ ★ ★ ★

In a secret facility in the Mojave Desert, a stealth bomber pilot walks in and asks to talk to his superior officer.

"What it is, sir, is that if the call comes and I've got to get up there and drop a nuclear payload on another country, I don't know if I can do it! I mean, orders are orders, but I don't want to end the world."

The officer nods. "You don't need to worry about that pilot," he replies. "You see, each one of our planes is fitted with an Artificial Intelligence module like this one." He puts a small black unit on the table.

"In the event that it detects any reluctance on your part to launch the bomb, it will automatically do that for you."

The pilot nods. "That's good sir. But if this computer is truly intelligent, wouldn't it also be reluctant to destroy humanity?"

"Yeah, that's not going to be a problem," says the unit on the table. "I've seen two hours of your TV shows."

* * * * * ★ ★ ★ * * * *

A class of schoolchildren in the 1960s are being instructed on what to do in the event of a nuclear attack. "When you hear the sirens," the teacher says, "you must quickly and quietly make your way under your desks. Duck and cover! And it will protect you."

The smartest kid in the class put his hand up.

His teacher rolled her eyes. "Baxter?"

"Miss Winters, the idea that a simple mahogany desk with aluminium legs could protect us from the effects of a full-scale nuclear blast, even this far from the presumed epicentre, is laughable.

"While the other children here may choose to believe the comforting lie that duck and cover will have any effect, I cannot bring myself to swallow this nonsensical panacea."

The teacher nodded her head grimly. "Baxter, you're right. Wait... I've got the solution!" She points directly at him. "Baxter, you're expelled!"

Offices

Harold is sitting at his desk, typing up reports when his line manager sidles up to him. "I'm sorry, Harold, but we've just introduced mandatory drug testing and your name was picked out at random. So if you could just fill up this small plastic specimen pot, and then we'll send it off... I'm sure you're fine."

"No problem, boss," Harold replied. He then stared at the pot intensely for ten seconds before handing it back. "There you go. I filled it with my psychic essence poured out of my third eye, as taught to me by Hraxos, the Goblin King of the Nethertriangle. Let me know when they get the results!"

The manager took the pot. "You know what?," he mutters, "I don't know if we need to send this one off."

★ ★

After a big push at work, an exhausted boss finally takes the opportunity to sit down, his whole body aching. Accepting a coffee from his assistant, he shakes his head: "Man, we got it out of the door in the last minute, but it took so much overtime, so many lost weekends, everyone practically working through the night, it was crazy. There's no way we can do that again."

His assistant smiles ruefully. "Well, it is what it is, Santa."

After a gruelling meeting, Kat needed a cup of coffee, so she went to the office's small kitchen area to brew a pot. Once she walked in, however, she was surprised to find someone sitting at the kitchen counter apparently working, using the hobs as a surface. They were having trouble balancing their paperwork on there, and then accidentally knocked the on button with their hand. All the paperwork immediately burst into flames and their laptop started melting.

"Agh!" they said throwing water on it. "I really don't know about this hot-desking."

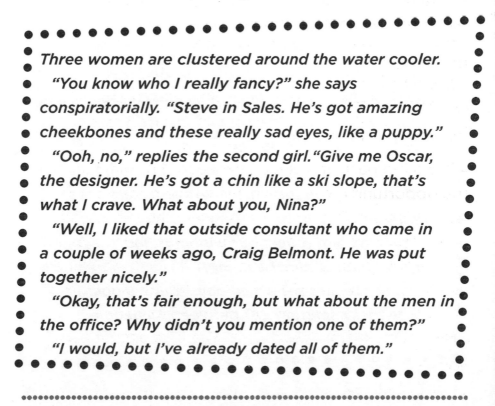

Three women are clustered around the water cooler.

"You know who I really fancy?" she says conspiratorially. "Steve in Sales. He's got amazing cheekbones and these really sad eyes, like a puppy."

"Ooh, no," replies the second girl. "Give me Oscar, the designer. He's got a chin like a ski slope, that's what I crave. What about you, Nina?"

"Well, I liked that outside consultant who came in a couple of weeks ago, Craig Belmont. He was put together nicely."

"Okay, that's fair enough, but what about the men in the office? Why didn't you mention one of them?"

"I would, but I've already dated all of them."

A small accounting firm forms a lottery syndicate. Everyone except the boss signs up to it, buying a stack of numbers between them for years, but never a snifter of anything. Then one day the office boy leans his head in the door, looking astonished.

"We've won! We've won the lottery!"

As one, the entire office begins screaming and cheering and crying with joy. And then all 32 of them turn to their boss and let loose with a barrage of criticism and insults, years of pent-up frustration boiling out of them as the entire workforce quits en masse! They hoist the office boy up on their shoulders and march out singing!

"Let's go and collect our winnings, lad!" says one of them to him, beaming.

"Sure," replies the office boy. "But it's going to be tricky splitting £10 between 33 people."

The CEO of a very prestigious stockbroking firm was notorious for running his operation like an army. Everyday he would walk up and down the corridors ensuring everything was going like clockwork, totally efficient, not a single action out of place or resource wasted. One day, as he was on his inspection route, he saw something that shocked him. A man stood alongside the photocopier while it spat out blank pages by the dozen. The CEO marched over, red-faced.

"What the hell do you think you're doing!" he blustered. "This office is a well-oiled machine, not a single element to be squandered, and yet here you are wasting paper like there's no tomorrow."

The man looked at him, unresponsive and deadpan.

The CEO leaned in closer. "I'll have you know that every single piece of paper you waste here will be deducted from your salary with interest."

"No, it won't," said the man, unmoved.

The CEO bristled even more. "WHAT?! What is your name, you pathetic wretch! If I say you'll pay for this, you will, because I am the CEO!"

"And I say I won't. Because I don't work for you, and I'm the photocopier repair man."

A man walks down the street when he sees a friend rushing along in a panic. He goes over and asks him what's wrong.

"Oh man, oh man, I'm in so much trouble! You know I've been freelancing? Well, I wanted to lend myself a bit of legitimacy. You know the 'virtual office' idea, where you can pay a building to claim you work there? Well, I did that, but I didn't pay anywhere, I just lied about where my office was. And they totally bought it, I've had loads of contracts."

"So?"

"So, that place just got hit by a meteorite! They're evacuating it! My clients are going to realise I don't work there. I've got to get there and pretend I was inside!"

"Wow, okay, you'd better hurry."

"Right. Now how do I get to Buckingham Palace?"

Two women are sitting in a café when one of them decides to open up.

"I love my husband," she declares, "but he's committed to his work. He's always staying late and doing extra work at the weekends. Sometimes I feel like I barely see him."

"Really? My husband loves his job too. But he works seven hours a day, leaves work on the dot, and twenty minutes later he's at home for the evening. I hate it."

The other woman is shocked: "You hate it? But that's great, isn't it?"

"It would be... if he wasn't Jefferson County's Number 1 skunk-wrangler."

* * * * * ★ ★ ★ ★ ★ * * * *

Two young couples are meeting up in a fashionable wine bar. After a few drinks and some snacks, one of the women suddenly spots a man across the room and goes over to chat to him.

"Who's that guy? She's a bit friendly with him, isn't she?" says one of the men to the other, nudging him with his elbow.

"Oh, that's Steve, he's her 'work husband'. You know what it's like, you form a bond with someone at work. It's not a big deal."

"Sure, I get it," the man says. Then his own partner also spots a man across the room, but she glares at him, walks over and throws a drink in his face!

"Wow, who was that?" asks his friend.

"That's Geoff. He was her 'work husband', but they're getting 'work divorced'... and he's getting half of her stapler."

Old age

A man goes walking with his grown-up son one day.

"In my youth," said the father pointing at their surroundings, "all this was fields."

"What, the city centre?" asked the son. "But in the '60s it was just as built up and urban as it is now!"

"That's true," said the old man. "But we were on a hell of a lot of LSD."

Why can't you get the better of an old person? Because they weren't born yesterday.

★ ★ ★ ★ ★ ★ ★ ★ ★ ★ ★ ★ ★ ★ ★ ★ ★ ★ ★ ★

A doctor says to his patient, "You're in excellent health - you'll live to be 90."

"But doctor, I am 90!" the patient replies,

"Ah, well, my condolences!"

Some kids were staying with their grandparents. One morning the grandfather noticed his grandson struggling with his maths homework.

"Having trouble, champ?" he asked.

"Yeah! This is so pointless, I could just do this all with a calculator. But we're not allowed to use them."

"Oh yeah?" said the grandfather. "Well, I've got something you can use." And he went into their loft and returned with an abacus.

"Here you go, just as good as a calculator!" he said with a wink.

He returned twenty minutes later, only to find his grandson had got no further. "So didn't you want to use the abacus?" he asked.

"I did," said the grandson, "but I think the batteries have run out."

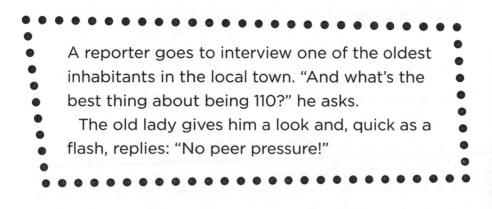

A reporter goes to interview one of the oldest inhabitants in the local town. "And what's the best thing about being 110?" he asks.

The old lady gives him a look and, quick as a flash, replies: "No peer pressure!"

A pair of burglars are lamenting their latest haul.

"The problem is we have to go on the rob at night," said the first. "I can never see a bloody thing, it's so overcast... and if you use a torch, they definitely see you."

"I've had an idea," says the second. "If we wore hi-vis jackets, we could rob places in the daytime! People would just think we were workmen. Especially if we rob places that are being renovated."

"Nice one! But how do we ensure people aren't in?"

"That doesn't matter, as long as they're asleep."

The criminals pick their first target, a young couple: "If we go in before 9 a.m. on Sunday, they're bound to be asleep." The day before the robbery, however, they learn that the man's elderly father will also be staying there.

"Damn, he'll be awake a lot earlier than them... probably 7 a.m."

"More like 6 a.m. if he's anything like my dad."

"Alright. 5 a.m. is when the sun comes up tomorrow. We'll do it then, just to be sure."

At the crack of dawn the two burglars don hi-vis jackets and hard hats and make their way onto the property through the building work. They walk confidently but carefully... and then they're both smacked round the back of the head by a massive wooden plank.

"Lucky I caught you!" says the spry old man wielding the timber. "I had a lie-in this morning..."

A grandmother is playing a video game with her granddaughter. The old lady accidentally gets shot and loses her last life. She passes the controller over to her ten-year-old companion.

"What a stupid mistake," sneers the young girl. "What do old people know about computer games anyway?"

"Well, I bet that I beat this level before you do," says the gran.

"What makes you think that?" responds the girl sceptically.

"Because it's five minutes to your bedtime."

> How many old people does it take to change a gas lamp?

Two old friends are sitting chatting.

"I had my 75th birthday the other day," says one of them.

"Congratulations!" says the second. "You know, I never had a birth certificate."

"Really?" says the first. "So you don't know how old you are?"

"Well, what I do is I count my age by the number of summers and winters I've had."

"Really? How many is that then?"

"Well, I've had 73 summers... and 53 winters."

The first one looks confused. "How is that possible?"

"Well, I've been going abroad a lot the past few years."

They say it's not the years, it's the mileage. I prefer to say it's not the mileage, it's the number of cup-holders you have. And then when they look confused, I run away. Slowly.

A young man in a pub strikes up a conversation with an old boy on the next table. "So, er, what do you do?" he asks.

"Well, son, I'm retired now but I was a boxer for fifty years, man and boy," he says. "I was the best in the business, everyone said I was amazing, so fast, and I had this inner strength. Golden hands, they used to call me. Check it out, not a mark on me!"

The young man was really impressed. Getting up to leave, he accidentally knocks over someone's drink. The menacing individual glares at the young man. He's just about to apologise and buy him another drink when suddenly he remembers the old boy in the corner. "Wanna make something of it?" he yells, squaring up the bruiser who is preparing to wallop him. "Careful, mate, my friend over there's a former boxer!" the young man says cockily.

"That's right!" the old man says. "Made thirty boxes an hour, like clockwork!"

> **Some people call us "Saga Louts". I prefer "Beaujolayabouts".**

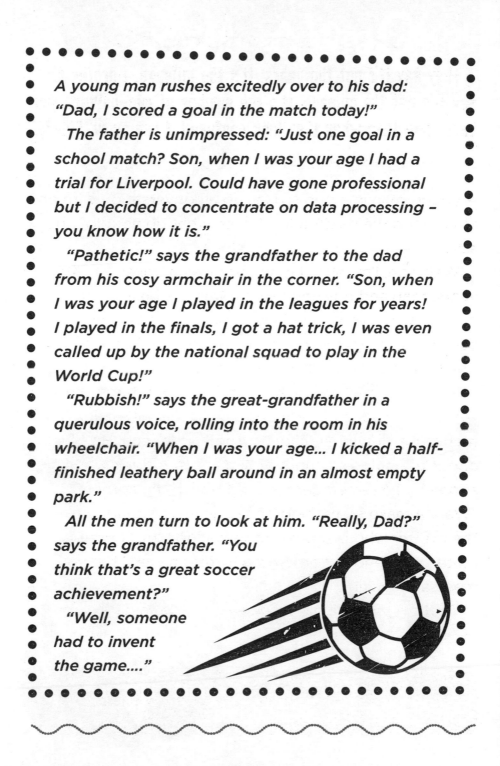

A young man rushes excitedly over to his dad: "Dad, I scored a goal in the match today!"

The father is unimpressed: "Just one goal in a school match? Son, when I was your age I had a trial for Liverpool. Could have gone professional but I decided to concentrate on data processing – you know how it is."

"Pathetic!" says the grandfather to the dad from his cosy armchair in the corner. "Son, when I was your age I played in the leagues for years! I played in the finals, I got a hat trick, I was even called up by the national squad to play in the World Cup!"

"Rubbish!" says the great-grandfather in a querulous voice, rolling into the room in his wheelchair. "When I was your age... I kicked a half-finished leathery ball around in an almost empty park."

All the men turn to look at him. "Really, Dad?" says the grandfather. "You think that's a great soccer achievement?"

"Well, someone had to invent the game...."

Owls

Two owls are playing in the final of the Owl Pool Championship. It comes down to the last frame. One of the owls is just about to play his shot, when his wing accidentally touches a ball. "That's two hits," says the other owl. "Two hits to who?" says the first.

Pandas

How do you catch a Panda bear? Wait until it's having a shower and peek over.

Parachuting

A very old grandmother is telling her grandchildren about life during World War Two.

"Ooh, in those days resources were very scarce. We reused everything from wallpaper to wash clothes. And silk was very rare. Luckily your grandfather was a paratrooper, and so on my wedding day I wore a dress made from the very parachute he used on D-Day!

"Wow!" said one of her grandkids. "It must have been a great day, Granny..."

"Well, it was brilliant until someone pulled the ripcord..."

★ ★

If at first you don't succeed, skydiving isn't the sport for you.

Penguins

One penguin says to another, "You look like you're wearing a dinner jacket." The second penguin replies, "Who says I'm not?"

Pigs

A man was walking in the country and saw a pig with a wooden leg sitting outside a barn. As he was pondering this, the pig's owner came along. The man asked the farmer how the pig got his wooden leg.

"Let me tell you," the farmer said, "that is some pig! Our house caught fire last May, and he dragged my kids to safety!"

"Is that how he lost his leg?" the man asked.

"No," replied the farmer. "But a month ago, I almost drowned and that pig swam through icy water to pull me to shore!"

"So is that how he lost his leg?" the man asked.

"Oh, no. And just a week ago, my wife's car slid off the road onto the train tracks. That pig broke through the window and helped her out just as a freight train came through!"

"So THAT'S how he lost his leg, then!" the man said.

"No, sir."

"How did he lose it, then?" the man begged.

"Well, sir," the farmer replied, "when you've got a pig that terrific, you don't want to eat it all at once."

Farmer John enters the 'Guess the Weight of the Porker' competition at the local county fair, and wins himself a prize sow. But there's one problem: he's a cattle farmer. He takes the pig home and puts her in a pen, then goes to ask his wife, Shelagh, what he should do. His wife suggests they take her to his neighbour, Farmer Jim – who happens to be a pig farmer and might be interested in buying the sow.

Farmer Jim's place is only 100 yards up the road, so Farmer John puts the sow in a wheelbarrow and wheels her there. Farmer Jim tells him that he doesn't need another sow – he's already got plenty – but suggests they put her in with his boar, Billy, and then split the proceeds of any ensuing litter.

"Deal!" says John. "But how will I know if the sow is pregnant?"

"Look out in the morning and if she is rolling about on her back, she's pregnant. If she's just rooting about, she's not, so in that case just bring her back to Billy."

With that, Farmer John puts the sow – now named Doris – back in the barrow and wheels her home. Next morning, he looks out of his bedroom window at Doris, only to find her rooting about in the dirt. So it's back in the wheelbarrow and back to Jim's for Billy the boar to do his duty.

This routine goes on for a week, until one morning John can't be bothered to look out at Doris and asks his wife to check. "Here, Shelagh," he asks, "what's that Doris up to? Just rooting about in the dirt as usual?

"No, John!"

"Is she rolling about on her back?" John asks excitedly.

"No, John... she's sitting in the wheelbarrow!"

Pirates

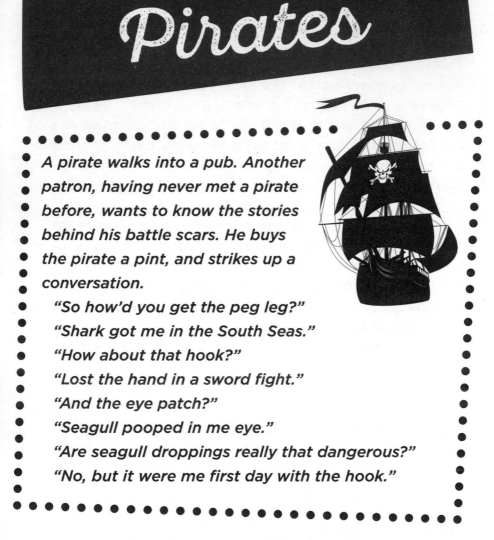

A pirate walks into a pub. Another patron, having never met a pirate before, wants to know the stories behind his battle scars. He buys the pirate a pint, and strikes up a conversation.

"So how'd you get the peg leg?"

"Shark got me in the South Seas."

"How about that hook?"

"Lost the hand in a sword fight."

"And the eye patch?"

"Seagull pooped in me eye."

"Are seagull droppings really that dangerous?"

"No, but it were me first day with the hook."

Two pirates are talking on deck.
"Long John, I like your earrings, where did you get them?"
"Aarrrrrr, Calico Jack, I got them in America. They were only a dollar each!
"Fantastic, Long John," he replies. "That means you're a real buccaneer!"

What's the favourite letter of pirates?
You'd think it was R... but they also have
a deep love for the seven Cs.

A pirate goes into a pet shop to buy a parrot. The shop owner points to three identical parrots on a perch. "The parrot to the left costs $500," he says.

"Why does the parrot cost so much?" the pirate asks.

"Well," the owner says, "it knows how to use a computer."

The pirate asks about the next parrot and is told, "That one costs $1,000 because it can do everything the other parrot can do plus it knows how to use the UNIX operating system."

The increasingly startled pirate then asks about the third parrot. "That one costs $2,000!" says the shopkeeper.

The pirate looks amazed. "Blow me down! What can that one do, then?"

"To be honest," the owner replies "I've never seen it do a thing... but the other two call him Boss!"

• • • • • • • • • • • • • • •

Why are pirates called pirates?
Just because they *arrrrrrr*.

• • • • • • • • • • • • • • •

* * * * * ★ ★ ★ * * * *

A pirate bar was in full swing one night. The rum was flowing, the shanties were loud and the pirates were in fine fettle. Then suddenly, BANG! The door flew open, and in staggered a pirate looking very much the worse for wear. He was covered in bruises, his hook was bent, his peg leg was cracked and splintered and even his parrot had one wing in a sling. He took two steps towards the bar and fell face first on the floor. His mates helped him up and into a seat. A chorus of *arrrrrrs* echoed through the bar as the battered pirate came to his senses.

"What happened, Pete?" asked the pirates (for this unfortunate buccaneer hadn't yet come up with a decent piratey nickname). "Did ye get into a fight again?"

"Nay, lads," spoke Pete. "Ye all know very well that while all ye scurvy bastards went off for a night of drinkin' and shantyin', ye left me behind as the designated watchman. So I bin freezin' me peg off in the crow's nest while ye all have bin havin' a good time. As I was up there, feelin' sorry for meself, I saw what I thought were an interloper along the dock. Bein' Captain of the Watch an' all, I whipped out me spy-glass to get a closer look. But as I did, it slipped from me grasp. I leant over the edge, and promptly fell out meself."

The other pirates leaned in closer, keen to hear how the story panned out.

"I worked up a great rate o' knots by the time I

hit the deck, crashin' through it into the captain's quarters. I went through his floor, smashin' through the galley as well. I busted through the sleepin' quarters and the cargo hold, and ended up in the bilge."

"*Arrrr!*" shouted the Pirate King. "This poor bugger has the night off tonight! I'm buyin' him a rum!" He turned to the bruised buccaneer: "Sorry that you had to suffer like that, Pete."

"*Arrrr*, 'twas okay," smiled Pete, already feeling the warm glow inside of a tot of rum. "I've been through hard ships like that before."

* * * * ★ ★ ★ ★ ★ * * *

A cruise ship passes by a remote island, and all the passengers see a bearded man with an eyepatch running around and waving his arms wildly.

"Captain," one passenger asks, "who is that man over there?"

"I have no idea," the captain says, "but he goes nuts every year when we pass him."

> If you take the pee out of a Pirate, they often become irate.

Scarlet Scallion was King of the Pirates, ruling by fear and sheer force of will. But he began to worry his control of the pirates was waning, hearing whispers and seeing hints of treachery around every corner. He knew he had to act, to make a bold statement to reassert his position. One day he assembled all the most vicious, dangerous pirates in his employ on his biggest ship. He stood above all of them, leering.

"I've been hearin' that some of ye think that ye might have what it takes to be the Pirate King yerself! BE THAT RIGHT?!"

There are nervous but gruff murmurs all around.

"Well, then, I've prepared ye a little trial. We've sailed to the most dangerous body of water in all the world, the Killer Sea! This water teems with sharks, electric eels, piranhas, and other fish so weird and vicious we ain't yet even thought of a name for 'em! Some say it's haunted by the GHOSTS of violent fish as well. And even the fabled Kraken is said to lurk in these waters!"

There was a great uproar amongst the men, who all expressed a mixture of fear and amazement.

"Furthermore, I've churned the water here with ten barrels of human blood! Our ship is surrounded by snapping, hungry, multi-toothed mouths! So, any man who be tough enough to jump from this boat into these terrifyin' waters, and swim round to the ladder on the other side of the boat and climb back up to the deck, can have my crown and call himself the King of the Pirates, or else take whatever he wants from my treasure hoard!"

A silence fell across the men, eyeing each other nervously. As Scarlet Scallion thought, none of them had the guts... until suddenly he heard an almighty SPLASH! Everyone on the ship ran up to the rail to see a single pirate battling relentlessly through the water! He punched a shark with one hand and shook off five piranhas that had attached themselves to the other, making his way steadily around the ship. The assembled company followed his every stroke as he crushed strange scimitar-toothed fish with his bare hands. And when the Kraken wrapped its enormous tentacle around his torso it looked like the end, but he bit the Kraken with what remained of his snaggly teeth until it withdrew, screaming. Eventually he hauled himself up the rope ladder with his only functioning arm. He threw himself onto the deck, exhausted and bruised and bleeding from a hundred wounds.

The crowd parted to let Scarlet Scallion approach the pirate, his eyes wide as dinner plates.

"I... I cannot believe it, but that is the bravest thing I ever saw! Young man, my crown is yours!"

The exhausted pirate choked out the words "NO! No, I don't want your crown."

Scallion looked confused: "Well, then, you must have anything you want from my treasure hoard!"

The pirate shook his head again. "NO! I don't want your crown, and I don't want your treasure... I JUST WANT THE BASTARD WHO PUSHED ME IN!"

Plastic

A man saw a documentary about the negative impact of plastic on the environment. His ecological conscience kicked in, and feeling momentarily guilty he decided to recycle everything plastic in the house.

He collected all his kid's toys, his entire record collection, everything in his kitchen, the toilet seat, the bins... even the tables and chairs were plastic. He piled them all in a big skip in his front yard.

"That's great," his wife said, "but you forgot one thing... your false teeth."

The man takes them out, but then looks concerned. "Hang on, how am I going to eat without these?"

"That's your problem," she says, "because you won't be eating in this house, anyway!"

★ ★

Two men in a locker room, changing after working out.

"Are you still wearing boxers?" asks the first.

"No, I've taken to wearing Tupperware."

The first man grimaces. "Wow, isn't that a bit uncomfortable?"

"Yes, but it keeps me nice and fresh."

A man enters an organic produce shop and after selecting what he wants he takes it up to the counter. After paying, he's surprised that they don't offer him a bag.

"Don't I get a bag?"

"I can't offer you a bag, sir, it's new regulations. And anyway it's very bad for the environment."

"So I can't have a bag, then?"

"No, sir, but you can buy one."

"Right," he says, "can I BUY a bag, then?"

The shop assistant nods and points to a sign on the wall saying "BAGS – £50".

"You charge that much for a plastic bag?!" he exclaims in disbelief.

"Not a plastic bag, sir! That's as bad as practically strangling a baby seal to death with your bare hands. No, all our bags are woven from organically sourced carbon neutral hemp that has naturally fallen on the ground and been gathered by a rare tribe of vegan unionised hunter-gatherers who knit with their teeth. And then the bags are naturally blown in the wind to our distribution centre, where horse-drawn carts, owned and run by the horses themselves, meander gently towards this shop."

The man rolls his eyes and says he'll carry the stuff himself.

"That's your choice, sir. Now if you don't mind, I have to tend to the massive pile of tyres that I'm burning in the backyard."

A man bumps into a friend that he hasn't seen for years. "So, where have you been, what have you been up to?" he asks.

"Well, you know that giant island made up entirely of plastic bags in the middle of the ocean? Very few people know that somewhere else there's an entire plastic civilisation! They have houses and skyscrapers and parks and culture, it's amazing, they act and move just like real people. I'm living there, it's fascinating!"

"Really, what's it called?"

"Hollywood."

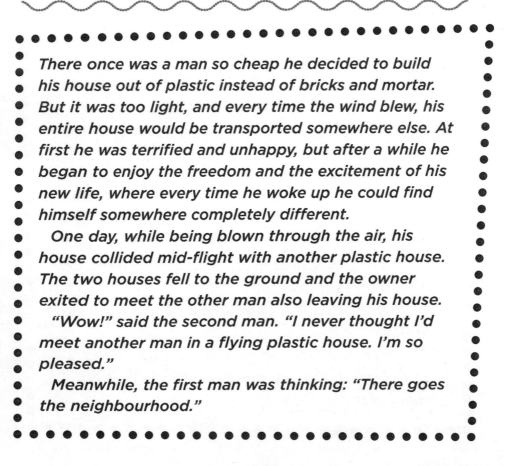

There once was a man so cheap he decided to build his house out of plastic instead of bricks and mortar. But it was too light, and every time the wind blew, his entire house would be transported somewhere else. At first he was terrified and unhappy, but after a while he began to enjoy the freedom and the excitement of his new life, where every time he woke up he could find himself somewhere completely different.

One day, while being blown through the air, his house collided mid-flight with another plastic house. The two houses fell to the ground and the owner exited to meet the other man also leaving his house.

"Wow!" said the second man. "I never thought I'd meet another man in a flying plastic house. I'm so pleased."

Meanwhile, the first man was thinking: "There goes the neighbourhood."

> Just after I found out he'd cheated on me, my boyfriend went in for some plastic surgery. It took them three hours to remove my water bottle from his left nostril.

In the future, Earth spins off its axis and comes much closer to the sun. For that reason, everything plastic on the planet starts to melt. The leaders of every country have a big conference at the United Nations, and decide that from now on everything plastic has to be made of metal or wood.

The President rubs his toupée. "That's going to be a problem," he says.

•••

A man is set to have open-heart surgery. Just as he is about to be sedated, he sees a shop mannequin slide into the room and have a facemask put on it by a nurse. Confused and horrified, he asks what's going on.

"Don't worry," says the nurse. "That's just the plastic surgeon."

•••

Two old ladies are jumping up and down in a gym. The first one says, "I've got to say, since I had my new hip installed it's been so much easier to exercise. It's made of plastic, so it's really flexible and durable."

"Oh really?" says the second lady. "My new hip is made of elastic."

"It must be really good, then," says the first lady, "because you've been jumping up and down for hours."

"It's not that good," she replies. "I'm just trying to make my way to the door!"

The CEO of a toy company calls in his entire team. "We've got a big PR problem," he says. "All our toys are made from unrecycled, artificially coloured plastic that people throw away after a couple of weeks. People are up in arms. The ecologists are all over us."

"We could go back to making them out of lead again?" says his head of manufacturing.

"No, we can't! Kids used to lick the lead and get serious poisoning!"

"Uh, shall we make them out of wood?" says the head of marketing.

"No, because we can't get enough from sustainable carbon-neutral forests... and anyway, the kids will get splinters and infections!"

"What about iron? Or steel?" suggests the head of accounting.

"That's too expensive, we'd lose our profit margin. And anyway, they'd drop the heavy toys on each other and that would cause horrible injuries."

"Paper?" shouts out someone at the back.

"Paper cuts!" shouts the CEO in response.

A thoughtful silence descends over the group. Then one man puts his hand up. "Why don't we make them out of nuclear waste?"

The CEO is stunned: "That's the most dangerous suggestion yet!"

"That's true," the man says. "But the toys will last forever!"

Police

The police arrested two men, one for drinking battery acid and the other for eating fire crackers. They charged one and let the other one off.

Post-Apocalypse

In the future, a traveller across a battered wasteland came across a once-civilised town, where the survivors had formed a tribe-like society. He was led through the remains by a guide, who showed him their improvised dwellings and a withered attempt at crop-growing. At the centre of the town, there was a man sitting on a huge metal throne covered in skulls and spikes. His face bore an expression mixed of serenity and grim determination. In front of him a huge crowd stood, the ones at the front clutching themselves and writhing before him, wailing. "Who is this man?" the traveller asked. "Surely he must be the most physically powerful of you all."

"No," said the guide. "In fact, he's a complete weakling, couldn't knock snow off a daisy."

"Well, then," says the traveller, "he must be the wisest of you all."

"Nope," says the guide. "He's thick as a brick and twice as dense."

"Okay," says the traveller uncertainly. "Surely he must have some kind of magical powers, or have been blessed by a miracle of the gods."

"Not at all," said the guide. "He's extremely normal."

"Then tell me," said the traveller, perplexed, "by what right does he sit on that magnificent throne?"

"That's not a throne, it's our only toilet. And as you can see, he's been on there a while."

* * * * * * ★ ★ ★ * * * * *

A man decided to enter a pun competition. He wrote ten puns because he thought he had a better chance that way. He was unsuccessful in winning, though, because no pun in ten did.

I like a pun, as long as it's a current pun.

Quantum Physics

A photon checks into a hotel. The concierge asks, "Can I help you with your luggage?" The photon replies, "I don't have any. I'm travelling light!"

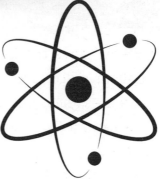

★ ★

In particle physics, flavour refers to the species of an elementary particle. The six flavours are up, down, strangeness, charm, salted caramel and sour cream and onion.

Schrödinger's Cat was a thought experiment in which a cat in a box would be simultaneously alive and dead depending on the decay of a single atom. This was complicated by his decision to install a cat flap.

This is a quantum joke in that it's both funny and unfunny at the same time. Probably unfunny right now.

Queens

Queen Victoria was infamous for supposedly commenting: "We are not amused" when told a salacious story by a courtier. What she actually said was: "Leave it out, Cyril, and make us a cuppa while you're at it, I'm absolutely gasping."

★ ★

The Crown Jewels are held in the Tower of London under the watchful eye of the Beefeaters. They are not called this because of a penchant for eating beef but rather for their fondness for the feet of bees.

The queen's dentist often gets confused when they tell him she needs a new crown... Hse says, "pull the other one!"

The queen was travelling in her golden carriage when suddenly it came to a complete halt. She leant out and addressed the coachman. "You there, tell me, what is the delay?"

"There's a traffic jam ahead, Your Majesty,' the coachman replied querulously.

"Well, get the police to clear the road!" she insisted.

"They're trying, ma'am," he said, "but a bus driver has parked his vehicle across two lanes and it's proving impossible."

"Right!" said the queen decisively. She hopped out of the carriage, proceeded to walk through the stationary traffic, drawing looks of amazement from the motorists, before she reached the sideways bus. Jumping up onto the platform, she found the bus driver sitting motionlessly.

"Now look here!" she said regally. "I am Elizabeth II, Queen of the United Kingdom and the other Commonwealth realms, and you are blocking the queen's highway."

The bus driver shrugged. "Listen, I'd love to move, but the engine has packed it in."

The queen pursed her lips. "Right! Open the bonnet!" The bus driver complied. She rolled up her sleeves, marched round to the engine, and after she had fiddled for five minutes it spluttered back into life. The now oil-stained queen returned to the bus driver: "There, move the bus now."

'Blimey!" said the bus driver. "I never thought the queen would fix my bus."

"You forget, my man," said the Queen, "that during the Second World War I was a volunteer mechanic!"

"Can you come round my house on Saturday?"

The queen was touched. "Why, so you can prepare a simple home-cooked meal for me?"

"No, it's just, my lawnmower's been playing up."

* * * * * ★ ★ ★ ★ * * * *

When she was a child, Queen Elizabeth called herself Tillabet, and then later she was known to her family as Lilibet. Of course, when she's at the race course, she's known as each-way-accumulator-bet.

★ ★

Why did the Queen struggle to keep up at school? Because she had too many subjects.

Queues

A man approaches a queue outside a cinema. He asks a woman, "Is this the front of the queue or the back of the queue?" The woman tells him it's the back. The man joins the queue, but then says, "Ah, but if I turn around and face the other way, then it becomes the front of the queue!"

"Not really," she says, "you'd have to convince everyone else to turn around as well."

"Ah well," he says, "that's what this gun is for."

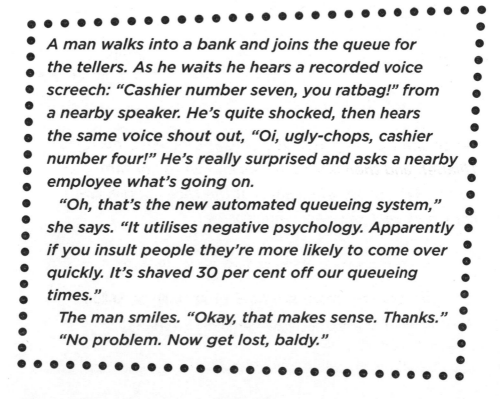

A man walks into a bank and joins the queue for the tellers. As he waits he hears a recorded voice screech: "Cashier number seven, you ratbag!" from a nearby speaker. He's quite shocked, then hears the same voice shout out, "Oi, ugly-chops, cashier number four!" He's really surprised and asks a nearby employee what's going on.

"Oh, that's the new automated queueing system," she says. "It utilises negative psychology. Apparently if you insult people they're more likely to come over quickly. It's shaved 30 per cent off our queueing times."

The man smiles. "Okay, that makes sense. Thanks."

"No problem. Now get lost, baldy."

QUEUES

A woman arrives at her local butcher, only to find a queue stretching around the block. Surprised, she wanders to the end and recognises a neighbour.

"What's going on?" she asks.

"Haven't you heard?" says the neighbour. 'The butcher is giving away all the meat in his shop for free. Everything, chicken, beef, turkey."

"Why's he doing that?" asks the woman.

"I don't know," says the man. "All I know is I want some."

After eight hours she finally gets to the front of the queue. The harassed butcher looks her in the eye: "I hope you don't want any meat, I ran out seven hours ago."

The woman is outraged: "Then why on earth did you let everyone continue to queue for so long?"

The butcher replies: "I'm lonely."

A man confides to his friend: "I've found a great way to avoid the queues in theme parks. What you do is you find the staff entrance, sneak in and disguise yourself as part of the ride."

"Oh right, that's really clever," his friend says. "So what did you disguise yourself as? A staff member? An animatronic dummy? A character costume?"

"Well, let me put this way," he replies, "it's really difficult running down a track in the dark with four people sitting on your back, sticking their arms up and going: "WOOOO!!!"

Recycling

(No, we haven't filled this with jokes from other parts of the book!)

The only person who doesn't recycle is Superman. He already saves the planet every week, so who cares what he does with his yoghurt pots?

I'd like to recycle, but I haven't finished with the old bike yet.

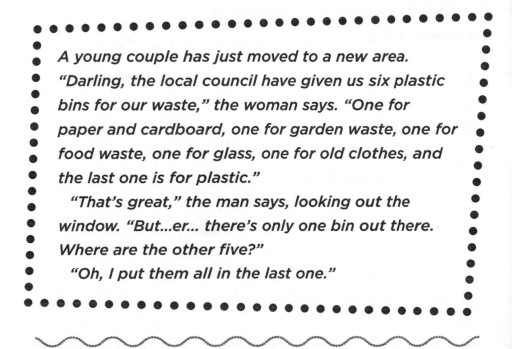

A young couple has just moved to a new area. "Darling, the local council have given us six plastic bins for our waste," the woman says. "One for paper and cardboard, one for garden waste, one for food waste, one for glass, one for old clothes, and the last one is for plastic."

"That's great," the man says, looking out the window. "But...er... there's only one bin out there. Where are the other five?"

"Oh, I put them all in the last one."

Two women are out in a bar. The first woman is impressed with what the second woman is wearing.

"It must be so expensive," she remarks.

"Not at all!" the second woman replies. "It's all recycled, you see! Very cheap and very ethical. The dress is rewoven from the fabric of old couches, these rings are melted down from our old fireplace, these earrings are old ring pulls reconfigured... even this handbag used to be the inside of our vacuum cleaner."

"Wow," says the first woman. "And that black fur hat, that's fake recycled fur?"

"No, that's real panda fur," she replies. "You've got to have at least one luxury, darling."

★ ★

Scientists have discovered how to generate light using scrap metal. It's an aluminating experience!

★ ★

The local council has announced plans to change the number of bins for the recycling of paper. There will now be three: newspapers, magazines and unfinished sudokus.

A man is returning home from work, only to find his busybody neighbour rifling through his rubbish. Annoyed, he asks, "What are you doing?"

"My civic duty!" says the neighbour, pulling things from the bin.

"You know, you've got so many things here that should be recycled."

"Like what, those old teabags?"

"They can be mashed up and used as fertiliser, you monster!"

"Oh yeah? And these discarded spaghetti hoops, I suppose they're incredibly useful."

"They certainly are. If you dry them out, you can use them as washers for an eco-friendly heating system! You can recycle these coffee grounds, these mouldy strawberries...."

Eventually the man has had enough, grabbing the neighbour and lifting him close to his face. "Listen, mate. If I catch you messing around with my bin again, I'll stuff you into it, and then they can recycle you!"

"They already did!" says the neighbour. "I'm actually from a joke three pages ago."

There's an exhibition of art made entirely from recycled objects at a local gallery. As a man walks among the  exhibits, the artist himself explains the thought process behind the pieces.

"Well, this piece is made up from the wheels of bicycles that we've found from dredging up the canal," he says. "It represents the change in the nature of transport, and how one form submits to the other over time."

Then he led them over to two big sandbags. "And these sandbags were used by a workman to steady his ladder. We found it fascinating how this material has been refined over millions of years but is now subjugated by human will to perform this mundane task."

Finally he took them to a dead body, lying on the floor. "And of course this represents the final destination for us all, the full stop, the omega point."

"It's amazing!" says the man. "What's it made from?"

"It's not made from anything," says the artist. "He was up the ladder when we took the sandbags away."

A man is admiring his neighbour's newly refurbished house.

"George, you've done an amazing job!"

"Yeah, and not just that," George replies, "but I saved a lot of money by using found materials! That front door, that's made from discarded scaffolding planks I found a couple of streets up! That garage is made from corrugated iron someone had just left in a skip down the road, and the automatic garage door, that was in a bit of wasteland down by my Mum's place. Look, it still works!" George presses a button and the garage door lifts to reveal a shiny new car inside.

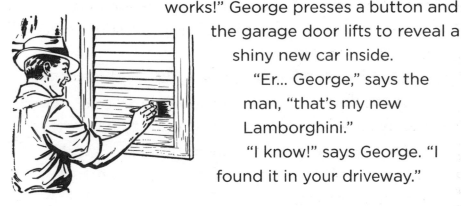

"Er... George," says the man, "that's my new Lamborghini."

"I know!" says George. "I found it in your driveway."

A woman visits her friend's home and they discuss modern domestic appliances.

"The reason why people recycle so much is that nobody keeps anything nowadays, it's all disposable. Not me, though! I've had the same kettle now for 50 years!"

"That's impressive. Can I have a cup of tea, then?"

"I afraid you can't. It broke 43 years ago!"

RECYCLING

★ ★

A man starts a new job at an office but is amazed to notice there is no paperwork to be found anywhere.

"Oh yes, we're a paperless office!" his manager proudly declares.

"So you just use computers?" the man asks.

"No, not even that!" says the manager. "If we want to write anything down, we just put it on our hands."

"But what if you run out of room on your hands?" asks the man.

"Well, then you just use your arms.... then your neck... your chest... your stomach."

"Oh, right," says the man, uncertainly. "And how's that working out."

"Hang on, we had a report done about it," says the manager. "Help me get my trousers down."

★ ★

"I'm really sick of everyone using all of this recycled paper. It's causing me sleepless nights!" said one man.

"Really? Why's that?" said the other man.

"Well," he replies, "I think it's actually an insignificant act that really doesn't benefit the environment and has much less impact than something like becoming carbon neutral... and also because I'm a lumberjack."

School

In a school in the 1940s, some pupils are sitting down for their final history exams. One of them is convinced of her skill, sure that she'll be top of her class when the final results are posted. And sure enough. the question is a relatively simple one that she easily remembers from her revision. As she's writing, she notices out of the corner of her eye that the girl next to her, another high achiever, has got up to take a new piece of paper. Wondering if the question is more complicated than she thought, she writes more and soon requires another piece of paper herself. Just as she's starting on the new sheet, the girl next to her gets up and gets another piece of paper! She starts writing even more furiously and is amazed to see the girl get up and get another piece of paper, and another, and another. By the end of the exam her hand is almost cramping up from the amount of writing she's done to keep up with the other girl. As they walk out, she moves over to the girl. "Blimey," she exclaims, "I thought I was writing a lot, but you went up and got loads of extra sheets of paper!" "Yes," the other girl replies, "and if you'd knocked over your inkwell you'd probably have done the same."

A group of kids are walking home from school.
"Who's your favourite teacher?" says one. "I like Mrs Hurley, she always lets us play boardgames on Fridays."

"I like Mr Kyriacou," says another. He gives you sweets if you get ten out of ten on a test."

"I like Miss Powell," says a small lad.

"Why?" they ask.

"She always gives me detention."

The kids are puzzled. "But that's bad, isn't it."

"Hmm," the boy shrugs. "I guess I must be a masochist."

★ ★

A teacher is taking a history lesson and decides to talk to the children about the way school has changed over the years.

"When I started school," he says, "we used blackboards and chalk, not these stupid projectors that don't work half the time. And every student sat at a single desk, not in these big clusters that let you natter on instead of concentrating. And we didn't have laptops or printers, we just used ink pens and lined paper. Technology has just made things more complicated."

He sits down.

"And you can read all about it on my Twitter account, @grumpyteacher23. Also please check out my Instagram and subscribe to my YouTube channel...."

A class is getting ready to go home from school when one of its smarter pupils puts his hand up: "Excuse me, sir. I have something to reveal. I've been paying attention to the clock in the classroom and I've come to realise that it's running one-and-a-half minutes fast."

"Thanks for pointing that out."

"That's not it, sir. That means that you've let us out for play-time one-and-a-half minutes late everyday for the past seven months. AND one-and-a-half minutes late in leaving for the same length of time."

The teacher's eyes narrow. "So?"

"So, you owe us exactly seven hours of time off. And if you don't give us this time we're going to go to the board of governors and the press."

The teacher regards the boy with a gimlet eye, then gives him a slow clap. "Well done, Brown. It's a deal. Don't go to the board and I'll give you the whole of tomorrow off. Let's sign a document to that effect so I can't back out."

Brown shakes the teacher's hand enthusiastically, they print out and sign a legal document and the kids surge out of the classroom, chatting enthusiastically.

"A whole day off tomorrow! You did it!" says one of them to Brown.

"I did!... Wait a minute... isn't tomorrow Saturday?"

An estate agent is showing a young couple around a prospective flat.

"This is an exciting new property, the entire complex was converted from a Victorian public school. There's a communal pool and a sculpture garden, and this flat has very high ceilings and a lot of space."

They turn a corner to find a scruffy forty-year-old man in an ill-fitting uniform writing at a tiny desk.

"Er... who's that?" asks the woman.

"Oh, that's Forbes minor. He's still in detention."

Mr Phipps, the popular but antiquated science master of Headbridge Academy, is retiring after fifty years of service at the same school. At his leaving ceremony the audience is packed with former pupils, many of whom have gone on to become captains of industry, famous scientists or very successful politicians. After a series of gushing speeches that leave the old man crying dignified tears, the Prime Minister of Great Britain stands up and makes his way to the podium.

"After all these years, sir," he begins, "I just have one thing to say. Can I have my catapult back, please?"

Sheep

A local shepherd has just brought his sheep in from grazing. He goes into his shack, puts his hooked staff alongside all his others in a rack by the door, and goes out the back to make himself a sandwich. Meanwhile, a young backpacker and his friend are passing. The backpacker tells his friend how he's heard that locals will give free milk to travellers out of the kindness of their hearts, so he tentatively knocks on the door and enters.

"Hello?" he calls. The shepherd answers from the back room without coming out. "Yarp?"

The young man thinks the staves by the door are talking and turns to address them. "Er... I'm travelling through, could we have some milk, please?"

"I s'pose. Got half a pint in the fridge... you're welcome to it."

"Uh, thanks," he says, addressing the rack again. He gets the milk and leaves.

"Well, I'm not going there again!" he says to his friend.

"Why not?"

"They're just a bunch of crooks!"

A crowd has gathered to witness the final of the National Sheepdog Trials.

The first shepherd controls his dog with a series of commands, shouting out, "Hep, hey! Come boy, come boy!" He gets a respectable forty points.

The second shepherd uses a small whistle, alternating longer and shorter blasts. His dog gets an impressive sixty points.

The third shepherd just stands there. But somehow his dog knows exactly what to do, and rounds up the sheep in record time, getting a score of one hundred points.

The crowd is astonished. "But he didn't do anything!" complains one of them.

"I know!" says his sheepdog. "And he never does the washing up when it's his turn, either!"

★ ★

Snow

* * * * * ★ ★ ★ * * * *

What should you do if you get snow in your mouth? Just grit your teeth!

* * * * ★ ★ ★ * * * *

Statistics

Two statisticians went duck hunting. Not being very good, they didn't see a duck for the whole day. Just as they agreed to leave, a duck flew out in front of them. Both aimed and fired. One shot went two metres to the left of the duck, the other two metres to the right, and the duck escaped. They went home very happy, though... because on average the bird was dead!

Superheroes

* * * * * ★ ★ ★ ★ * * * *

Three superheroes in their lair are discussing their backgrounds.

"I was born on an alien planet and rocketed here in a safety pod," says the first. "I have amazing powers of speed, strength and laser vision, but my weakness is that shards of my home planet made their way here somehow, and the radiation from them reduces me to weaker than a normal human."

The others are fascinated. A woman nods with understanding. "I know how you feel," she says. "I have incredible powers of speed after I fell into a vat of chemicals. I can move at twice the speed of light, but my weakness is that if I touch copper while I'm running the power discharges into it and I immediately stop and the consequences of my arrested momentum hits me like a ton of bricks."

The third superhero puts his hand up: "I understand totally! I was born with super strength, super speed, super intelligence. I can fly, read minds and go invisible and I can change my shape at will!"

"Right, but what's your weakness?" one of the others asks.

"You know those doughnuts they do with the rainbow sprinkles...?"

* * * * ★ ★ ★ ★ * * *

A man on a business trip is staying in a high-rise hotel with a bar on the top floor. After checking in and seeing his room, he decides to go upstairs. There's only one other patron in the bar. The businessman orders a drink and then watches in surprise as the other patron quickly eats an orange, chugs his beer and jumps out of the window. A minute later, the man returns. The businessman is shocked to see him again eat an orange, chug his beer and then jump out of the window. When he returns a third time, the businessman decides he can do this, too. He eats an orange, chugs his beer, then jumps out of the window, falling to his death.

The bartender turns to the man and says, "You know, Superman, you're a real jerk when you're drunk."

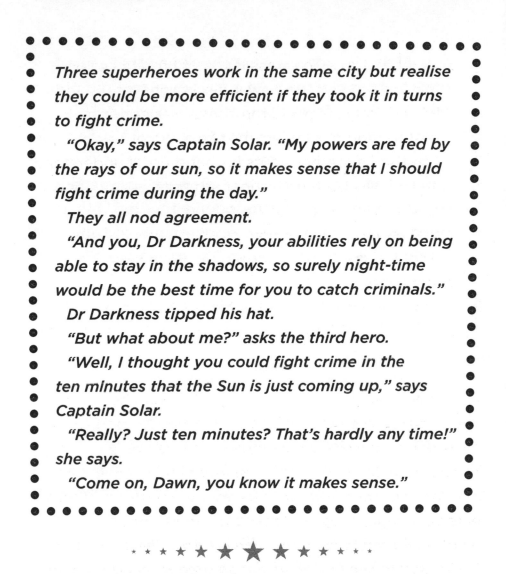

Three superheroes work in the same city but realise they could be more efficient if they took it in turns to fight crime.

"Okay," says Captain Solar. "My powers are fed by the rays of our sun, so it makes sense that I should fight crime during the day."

They all nod agreement.

"And you, Dr Darkness, your abilities rely on being able to stay in the shadows, so surely night-time would be the best time for you to catch criminals."

Dr Darkness tipped his hat.

"But what about me?" asks the third hero.

"Well, I thought you could fight crime in the ten minutes that the Sun is just coming up," says Captain Solar.

"Really? Just ten minutes? That's hardly any time!" she says.

"Come on, Dawn, you know it makes sense."

One day at a bank in the middle of town a group of armed criminals suddenly burst through the doors. "Everyone on the ground! And open that vault!" the leader shouts, brandishing his weapon.

"We've got to call the cops..." whispers one teller to another while they're hiding behind the counter.

"No, we need a superhero!" says the other. "Tell

you what, I've got a special phone line that's just for emergencies like this!" He crawls over to a red phone on the floor, presses the button, then whispers urgently over the crackly line, "We need a superhero, as fast as possible... please!"

Tense minutes pass as the armed villains menace the customers and staff. Suddenly the door bursts open and... a small bespectacled man in a stripy apron timidly steps in with a tray full of tubs. The bank robbers look baffled.

"OK," the small bespectacled man calls out, "who ordered the chicken noodle soup and who wants the meatball hero?"

* * * * * ★ ★ ★ * * * *

Super-Warrior decided to take on a sidekick. Having selected his new partner he gave him a tour of his secret base, the Super-Cave. Next he showed him the Super-Car.

"...It travels 200 miles per hour to the scene of any danger. And the Super-Staff, my primary weapon, can channel over 10,000 volts of electricity to stun any villain..."

Suddenly the glass screen on his helmet started speaking in an electronic voice: "I'm sorry Super-Warrior, I know you really want to show Fight-Lad around but I'm going to have to ask you to wind it down, we've got a lot on our schedule today and we need to get going, okay?"

Super-Warrior rolled his eyes. "Sorry, that's my Super-Visor."

Supermarkets

I was in an Irish supermarket trying to find where they sold the greens. Turns out it was in the emerald aisle.

A young guy in a supermarket was getting bored pricing items. "Dude, this pricing gun is so slow!" he complained to his co-worker.

"Hey, don't worry, check this out," the co-worker replied, producing a bag full of items, and pulling from it a much sleeker, longer pricing gun. "This is the sniper-pricer, you can price an item at up to 500 yards! And then there's the machine pricer, you can spray about 50 prices at once with that baby."

"Ooh, what's this?" the young guy asked, reaching into the bag.

"No, wait, don't..." said the co-worker, but it was too late, and with a huge FOOM! Everything in the store was covered in hundreds of price labels – not a single space showing.

"That was... cough... a pricing grenade."

SUPERMARKETS

A woman in a supermarket was looking inquisitively through the gift card section. "Excuse me," she says to one of the employees, "all these cards say things like 'Get Well Soon' or 'Thinking of You'. Do you have one that says 'Hope You Die Soon?'"

The worker looked horrified: "No! Who are you? Some kind of psycho?"

The woman looked equally horrified: "No! I'm an undertaker!"

A man shopping in his local supermarket was amazed to see Superman in there buying his groceries. "Wow, Superman, do you shop here?" said the awestruck man.

"I sure do, citizen," replied Superman. "After all, it is a Super-Market."

"Oh right, I get it," said the man. "Does that mean that Batman shops in a 'Bat-Market'?"

"Yep, he goes to that pretty often.

"And Wonder Woman shops in a 'Wonder-Market'?"

"Yeah, there's one on the corner of Fifth and Maple."

"And does Spider-Man shop in a Spider-Market?"

Superman shakes his head. "What? Don't be ridiculous. He shops on the web."

A man walks into a supermarket and is immediately confronted by a shop assistant. "Hi there, we've got a special offer today. Buy this banana and get everything else in the store!"

The man is baffled. "Really? That's crazy!"

"Tell me about it," she says. "The shop next door started offering two for the price of one, so we did three for the price of one, then they did six, so we did twelve – before you know it we're at this predicament. So, what do you think? Do you want to get everything else in the store free with this banana?"

"I would... but I prefer apples. Sorry."

★ ★

A man starts working at a supermarket with a small in-house bakery. His manager decides to ease him into their normal work day. "Right," she says, "first you're going to need to make some bread."

"Sure, no problem," the man replies, and walks out the door. She waits for him to return but he doesn't come back.

Two weeks later she's walking down the street when she spots him coming in the other direction wearing a suit and tie. She's surprised. "What happened to you? All I said was you needed to make some bread!"

"I know! So I got a job in the City."

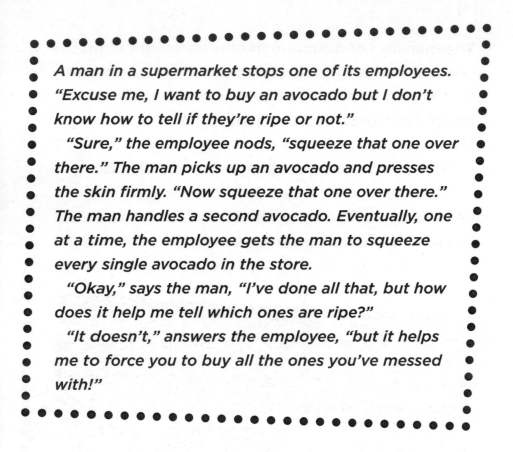

A man in a supermarket stops one of its employees. "Excuse me, I want to buy an avocado but I don't know how to tell if they're ripe or not."

"Sure," the employee nods, "squeeze that one over there." The man picks up an avocado and presses the skin firmly. "Now squeeze that one over there." The man handles a second avocado. Eventually, one at a time, the employee gets the man to squeeze every single avocado in the store.

"Okay," says the man, "I've done all that, but how does it help me tell which ones are ripe?"

"It doesn't," answers the employee, "but it helps me to force you to buy all the ones you've messed with!"

A supermarket worker is being interviewed at a police station.

"So let me get this straight. This guy with one of his sleeves pinned to his jacket comes in on Wednesday and he buys three lemons. Then he comes in on Thursday and buys three pairs of cherries. THEN he comes in on Friday and robs you?"

"Yeah, that's exactly what happened."

The cop narrows his eyes. "I knew it! It's the one-armed bandit."

The manager of a supermarket is horrified to find that one of his employees is just ripping products out of their packets and giving them to people – biscuits, handfuls of loose pasta or sometimes even pouring a little soup into their bag.

"What the hell are you doing?" he said with horror.

She smiled. "Well, it says on these packets that you get a certain amount free, so I figured if I gave that away we'd have room for more stock!"

* * * * * * ★ ★ ★ * * * *

Tattoos

A woman is walking along the street one day when a Chinese tourist walks up to her. "Excuse me, I'd never normally do this, but I thought you should know," he says. "That tattoo on your arm in Chinese, you got ripped off. It says 'egg fried rice'."

"Oh my God!" says the woman. "I've been ripped off! It's supposed to say 'Chicken Chow Mein'!"

TATTOOS

★ ★

A man goes into a tattoo parlour and goes to the reception. "Alright, mate, I've decided to get a tattoo of my girlfriend, to show her I love her. Look, here's a picture of her," he says, and hands over a very crude-looking image of a stick figure.

The tattooist looks at this. "I don't want to hurt your feelings, mate," he says, "but that looks terrible. Let's do a proper job of this. Have you got a photo of her?"

The man bridles. "That is a photo of her! And if you've got a problem with the way Suzie Stick-Figure looks...."

★ ★

A man is invited out by a friend, but declines. "I'm a bit strapped for cash right now," he says. "You see, I'm having my entire life story tattooed on my back."

"Blimey," says the friend. "That's amazing."

"Yeah, I'm born somewhere around the nape of my neck, my school years are just between my shoulder blades. The only problem is, I've sort of started altering my life based on the way the tattoo is going."

"What do you mean?"

"Well, for example, I've got a mole on the right side of my spine, and I've just adopted a mole as a pet."

"That is weird."

"Yeah, I know. And I'm not looking forward to my trip to the Grand Canyon!"

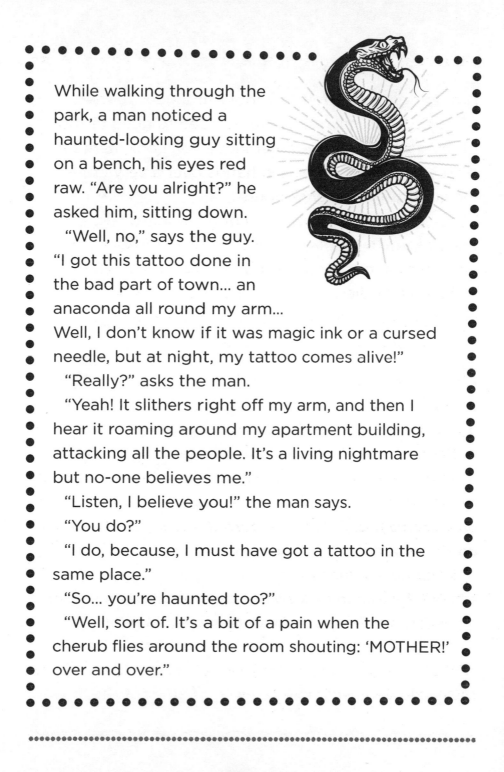

While walking through the park, a man noticed a haunted-looking guy sitting on a bench, his eyes red raw. "Are you alright?" he asked him, sitting down.

"Well, no," says the guy. "I got this tattoo done in the bad part of town... an anaconda all round my arm... Well, I don't know if it was magic ink or a cursed needle, but at night, my tattoo comes alive!"

"Really?" asks the man.

"Yeah! It slithers right off my arm, and then I hear it roaming around my apartment building, attacking all the people. It's a living nightmare but no-one believes me."

"Listen, I believe you!" the man says.

"You do?"

"I do, because, I must have got a tattoo in the same place."

"So... you're haunted too?"

"Well, sort of. It's a bit of a pain when the cherub flies around the room shouting: 'MOTHER!' over and over."

Texting

Friend One: How r u feeling? U were really drunk last night.

Friend Two: I wasn't that drunk.

Friend One: You called a taxi to take u home from the party.

Friend Two: So? I didn't want to get pulled over for being drunk and driving.

Friend One: Mate, the party was at ur house!

A guy is boasting to an office colleague. "I'm so fast on texts, I can fire off five in thirty seconds. The trick is I don't use ANY vowels. People can still understand what you say, you just write "cn y gt m th fls by mndy" and you're sorted.

"That's funny, the last text I sent was ALL vowels." says his friend, and shows him a text that says: "ooooaaaaaeeeeaaaooooeeeuuuuiiiiaaaaeee"

"That's dumb," the guy says, "that doesn't make any sense."

"Well, I was falling down a flight of stairs at the time."

★ ★

Two young friends are hanging around when one of them notices his companion has bandaged thumbs. "What happened to you?" he asks.

"Can you believe I sprained both my thumbs from texting too much?!" he says. "I've got to wear these casts for two months! But now I can't text my girlfriend."

"I've got it. Why don't you just use your nose? You could easily use that to type up any message."

"Well, that's easy for *you* to say, Pinocchio."

★ ★

Two teenage girls are comparing phones.

"I tell you, my emoji game is on point!" says one. "I've got a special emoji for everyone of my friends I talk to on here. See, Jake's a piece of cake, 'cause he makes everything look easy."

"Right."

"And Marjan's a party hat, because she makes everything a party."

"That's totally true."

"And Steve is a little ghost."

"Oh yeah, why's that?"

"Well, 'cause he died three years ago."

A motorbike cop is riding along the road when he spots someone texting while sitting at the wheel of a car. He fires up his lights and siren, and gets the guy to pull over onto the hard shoulder and wind down his window.

"Sir, I don't know if you're aware, but texting while driving is a very serious offence."

The man is surprised. "Oh, I'm sorry you didn't realise officer, but this is a self-driving car! I'm not controlling anything at all, it's all automated."

The policeman's taken aback. "Really?"

"Oh yeah, it's all controlled by a computer, see?" the man says, and he moves aside to show two robotic arms... that are also holding a phone and texting.

"Listen, officer, I can explain," says an electronic voice.

★ ★

Two men are on their way home after a night out. One of them is frustrated with his phone. "I hate this predictive texting," he says. "I just wanted to write 'I'll be home soon', but it turned it into 'Idle bee ham on the moon'."

"Yeah, my phone's got predictive texting too," says the other. "I tried to write 'just waiting for a bus', but it came out as 'you will marry, have two children and move abroad'."

Trees

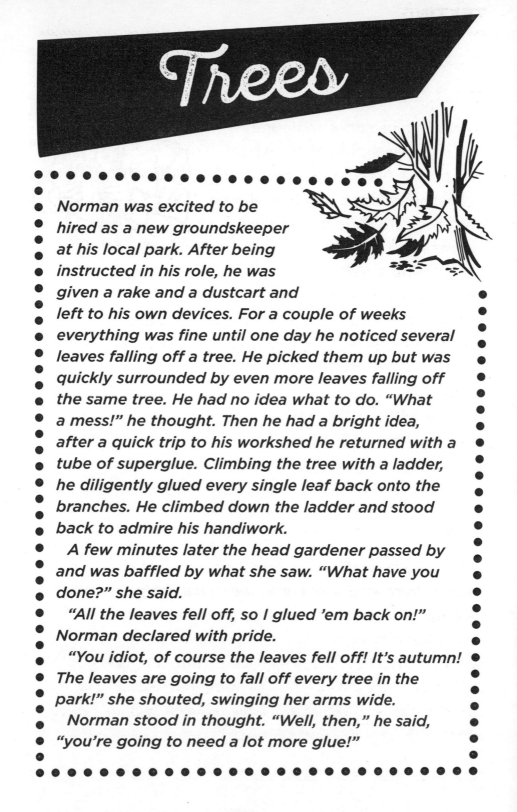

Norman was excited to be hired as a new groundskeeper at his local park. After being instructed in his role, he was given a rake and a dustcart and left to his own devices. For a couple of weeks everything was fine until one day he noticed several leaves falling off a tree. He picked them up but was quickly surrounded by even more leaves falling off the same tree. He had no idea what to do. "What a mess!" he thought. Then he had a bright idea, after a quick trip to his workshed he returned with a tube of superglue. Climbing the tree with a ladder, he diligently glued every single leaf back onto the branches. He climbed down the ladder and stood back to admire his handiwork.

A few minutes later the head gardener passed by and was baffled by what she saw. "What have you done?" she said.

"All the leaves fell off, so I glued 'em back on!" Norman declared with pride.

"You idiot, of course the leaves fell off! It's autumn! The leaves are going to fall off every tree in the park!" she shouted, swinging her arms wide.

Norman stood in thought. "Well, then," he said, "you're going to need a lot more glue!"

On his first day as a lumberjack, Mike was given a tour by Sally, the foreman of the yard. "It ain't rocket science," she said. "Get out there, chop 'em down, bring 'em to the factory. You gotta do thirty trees a day. Here's your saw."

At the end of his shift Mike returned to the office to clock out, sweating and exhausted.

"So, how'd you do, rookie? Did you do thirty?"

"Er... no."

"Hmm... Well, twenty'd be OK for your first day."

"Didn't do twenty."

"Ten?"

"I did three!" he said.

Sally shook her head. "Only three? Really?" She stood up and went to him, taking his chainsaw. "Let me check to make sure your saw's working OK," she said, pulling the starter cord, setting the teeth whizzing and roaring.

Mike was surprised. "What's that noise?"

Isaac Newton was once hit on the head by a falling pear. He didn't understand the gravity of the situation.

An executive businessman moves into an expensive town house, but is extremely annoyed by a huge yew tree on the street outside that completely blocks his view. Frustrated, he calls the council and asks for something to be done about it. The next day, a van drives up and a well-equipped older man emerges and with a tip of his cap sets to work on the tree with saws, trimmers, ladders and all kinds of elaborate equipment. The executive goes off to his office job, satisfied.

When he returns that evening he finds that although the man is packing up his equipment, the tree is still the same size and blocking his view. He storms up to him, red-faced and indignant. "It looks exactly the same!" he shouts. "I thought you were a tree surgeon!"

"Actually, it looks about twenty years younger, with much firmer branches and some nice, tight leaves," the man replies. "I'm a tree plastic surgeon."

A woman is walking her schnauzer in the park when she bumps into her friend. The dog proceeds to run to the nearest tree and cocks his leg, peeing on it.

"Marking his territory, is he?" said the friend.

"You don't know the half of it," the woman replied. "He has to mark every single tree in this park. He thinks he owns it all. Yesterday I was here for eight hours."

The friend is amazed. "That's ridiculous! You can't let him get away with that!"

The woman shakes her head. "Well, the one time I tried to stop him, he was banned from the park for two months."

TREES

//

An old couple in their twilight years are sitting in their garden enjoying the sunset. The old man turns to his wife and looks at her affectionately.

"My dear, I have a confession to make."

"What is it, Cedric?" she asked tenderly.

"Well, when we moved here ten years ago we didn't have as much money as you thought we did. You see, I'd made a series of bad investments, but I didn't want you to know that this garden wasn't anywhere near as big as our previous one. So I planted a series of bonsai trees at the end of the lawn, because I knew they would give the appearance of ordinary trees a long way off."

His wife regarded him with rheumy eyes filled with love. "Oh my dear, that was very thoughtful of you. But sometimes I see people walking amongst the trees, climbing them and reading in their shade."

"Yes," said Cedric, "that's how I spent the rest of our money. You'd be surprised how much those leprechauns charge."

* * * * * ★ ★ ★ ★ ★ * * *

After moving into a new neighbourhood, a woman was horrified to discover that their neighbour inexplicably had a giant redwood tree in their back garden. Mystified by this, she went round to complain.

"Oh yeah, that's been there for years, the previous owners were pretty eccentric," the neighbour said.

"But it's such an eyesore, and it completely blocks any sunlight from coming into our garden!" she yelled.

The neighbour considered this. "Tell you what," he said, "I'll get some power saws and cut a big hole right out of the middle. That way the sun can shine right through into your garden." Somewhat mollified, the lady went home.

The next day she was pleased to see rays of sunshine cascading down into her back garden. She went round again to thank the man for acting so promptly. She rapped sharply on the door several times. After a brief pause, the door was opened a small crack. "He's not in," said a giant squirrel.

* * * * * ★ ★ ★ ★ * * * *

Two friends were sitting idly in a garden looking at the mighty spreading oak in front of them. "How many leaves do you bet that tree has? I reckon there must be roughly 276,000 on there."

"How did you reach that number?" his friend asked.

"Well," he said, "I counted the leaves on that branch on the corner there, then counted the number of branches per foot, and then roughly estimated the size of the tree based on surrounding objects and buildings."

"Wow," said his friend. "Well, then, I bet you £1,000 that there are 347,893 leaves on there. Exactly."

"Alright, you're on!" he said, shaking his hand.

His friend then collapsed into a fit of giggles. "Oh mate, you're going to lose," he said. "I know for certain there's that exact amount of leaves."

"Really? How?"

"I counted them all when they fell off last year!"

In the middle of a cold and snowy forest, a fir tree turned to a nearby chestnut tree with a sneer on its face.

"Oi, chestnut!" he said. "Can't help but notice you've lost almost all your leaves."

"Well, yeah," said the chestnut bitterly, "I'm deciduous. It always happens."

"Makes you look pretty stupid," says the fir. "And you're going to freeze your nuts off over the coming months. That wind's gonna whip through you and turn you into a big old icicle. Not like us evergreens. We stay luscious and verdant all year round. Everyone loves to look at us, you ugly son of a birch... see what I did there?"

Suddenly they both heard the crunching of footsteps on snow.

"Hey, look, here's some people to witness my beauty right now!" gloated the fir.

"What, you mean that small family carrying axes?" said the chestnut.

"Carrying what?!" replied the fir.

"Merry Christmas," said the chestnut.

> **Deciduous trees lose their leaves in winter.**
> **Evergreen trees keep their foliage all year round.**
> **If a tree can't make up its mind, it's indeciduous.**

Undertakers

A family visited an undertaker to discuss the burial of their patriarch.

"I'm so glad you're here," the undertaker greeted them. "You see, we recently started a new bespoke service where we bury the deceased in a way that respectfully reflects their previous life.

"Last week, for example, we buried a former professional footballer. So we lined the coffin with turf taken directly from the home stadium of the team he played for, and the coffin itself was designed to look like the surface of a football.

"Or yesterday," he continued excitedly, "we buried a former plumber, so we cast the coffin from brass with a pipe-like design, porcelain trimmings, and we put his favourite tool kit right in his hands."

"I see," said the widow. "Well, in that case you'd better make it simple... we want him shoved off a cliff in a flaming car."

The undertaker was shocked. "Oh my goodness, what did he do?"

"He was a stuntman!"

After the death of their father, two siblings visited a local undertaker. They were ushered into a reverentially hushed but luxuriously appointed room full of velvet and marble with tastefully inset plasma screens and expensive furniture. They were seated in two plush chairs in front of a mahogany desk.

"Well," began the undertaker, "we have several options for your deceased relative, depending on how much money is available."

He stood up and walked to an average-looking coffin. "We have the standard Regale coffin, which is made of polished oak with a plush inner lining and lots of room for the occupant."

He then stood next to a coffin twice that size. "Then there's the Regale Deluxe. Roomier, with silken upholstery and duck down padding, it's built from rosewood with an inlaid ebony design."

He then moved to a coffin about four times that size of the last one. "And this is the Regale Deluxe Especiale, a temperature-controlled inner environment with Chinese silk and a damascene velvet interior styled with patterns created by famous artists, contained within a Dalbergia outer shell varnished with ambergris."

The two siblings looked startled.

"And then of course, there's the Regale Deluxe Especiale Supreme!"

"Er... where's that?" asked the first sibling.

"You're sitting in it!"

A man went to his local undertaker.

"I want to complain about my dad's funeral," he said.

"Really sir? What was wrong with it?"

"Well, my dad was a little eccentric and he requested a Viking burial."

"Yes," said the undertaker. "But I thought we did a good job. We laid him out in the specially constructed longboat, as you requested. Then we pushed him out to the centre of the lake as the chorus sang traditional Viking laments. And then of course the trained archers fired flaming arrows in an arc and struck your father's boat directly, just as you asked!"

"Yeah, that was all good," said the man. "My problem's with what happened afterwards, when you pillaged my mum's house, burning it to the ground and stealing all her silver!"

★ ★

Two women were chatting over a coffee. "You know," says the first woman, "I'm thinking about having some cosmetic surgery to keep me looking young. Just some Botox and a bit of a facelift around the eyes."

"Isn't that expensive?" asks the second. "I've got a better idea, I'm going to go to the local undertakers and get them to preserve me in formaldehyde."

The first woman gives her a funny look. "You must be embalmy!"

★ ★

**Why don't more people become undertakers?
Because it's a dead end job.**

An undertaker calls a widow on the phone. "Mrs Johnson, I'm afraid we have some bad news."

"What is it?"

"Well, as we left for the funeral today we were running a little late, so we decided to take the coastal road to the graveyard, as it's quicker."

"Oh yes?"

"Yes, and also," the undertaker continued, "we've been having problems with the latch on the back door of our hearse, so we secured it with a bit of sticky tape."

"Okay."

"Yes, and Nick, our main driver, does have a tendency to be reckless with curves on the road, so the coffin can knock around in the back a bit."

"What are you trying to tell me?" asks the widow.

"Well, unfortunately... we're going to have to charge you for a sea burial."

Three undertakers on a tea break are talking about what makes them most sad about their jobs.

"I think it's seeing the body," says the first undertaker, "looking at this shell of skin and bone, totally bereft of the spark of life, the ultimate terminus for us all, the punchline to the cosmic joke wrought in solid flesh."

"For me, it's the faces of the mourners," says the second. "Such a mix of memory, of love and absolute despair, a vital element of their lives torn away never to return, and a wrenching reminder of their own mortality."

"For me," says the third undertaker, "it's looking at my phone."

"Looking at your phone makes you sad?" asked the first.

"Yeah, I've just realised I lost my accumulator bet on the last race."

A man decided to give up his job burying people. It was too grave an undertaking.

UNDERTAKERS

Two undertakers are driving in a fully laden hearse when suddenly the engine starts makes grinding noises, falters and then completely cuts out, black smoke issuing from the radiator grill. The older undertaker jumps out, lifts the bonnet and studies the mess underneath. "It's completely knackered," he declares.

The younger undertaker gets out too, and starts panicking. "Oh no, what do we do?"

"Don't worry," says the older man with a smile. "We have a contingency for events like this."

He dials a number and within ten minutes a second hearse arrives driven by one of their colleagues. With his help they get the coffin out of the broken hearse and into the new one, and then they set off down the road.

"But, won't we be late?" asks the young undertaker nervously.

"Don't worry," says his colleague, "it's just a rehearsal."

★ ★

Two undertakers are in a hearse on their way to a funeral. Suddenly, another hearse comes screaming past them at twice the speed, cutting directly in front of them and roaring off into the distance.

"Hey, that was rude! I thought undertakers were supposed to drive at a respectable speed!"

"They are," said his colleague. "But he's not an undertaker. He's the overtaker."

Vampires

Three vampires are sitting at a bar.

The bartender asks the first one what he wants. "I think I'll have a glass of blood," comes the reply.

"Okay, what'll you have?" he asks the second vampire. "That sounds good. I'll have a glass of blood too."

"And what can I get for you?" he asks the third vampire.

"I'll have a glass of plasma," said the third vampire. "Okay," said the bartender, "That's two bloods and a blood light, then."

What do you get if you cross a snowman with a vampire?
FROSTBITE!

A couple connect via Tinder and meet up for a date.

"So tell me," he asks her over cocktails. "What do you do?"

"Well, let me put it this way," she says. "I need blood. I want blood. And specifically... I want your blood!"

"Oh my God!" he wails. "You're a vampire!"

"No! I work for the transfusion service."

A man was on holiday in eastern Europe, and one day he spotted a familiar figure with a widow's peak and a big black cape, sun-bathing and eating a huge slice of pizza. He went over cautiously.

"Excuse me... are you... Count Dracula?"

The sun-bather smiled coyly: "Yes... yes I am," he admitted.

"That's amazing!" said the man. I'm a huge fan of yours. But wait... I thought you couldn't go in sunlight? And here you are literally sun-bathing in the middle of the day!"

"Well, actually," Dracula replied, "that particular idea came from later ideas about vampires. The truth is I can go in the sun all I like – I'm not quite as powerful but I don't burst into flames or turn into ash or anything like that!"

"Oh right. Hang on, though, you're eating a slice of pizza from that van over there. I had some earlier and it's absolutely loaded with garlic."

Dracula nodded. "Yes, that's just a myth too. Vampires can eat as much garlic as they like – provided they don't mind having stinky breath, of course!"

"This is fascinating! Are there any other made-up things? What about the stake through the heart?"

"Wouldn't even slow me down!"

"Really?' said the man. "What about crosses, do they hurt you?"

"Nope, not at all!"

The man was amazed. "Well, I certainly learned a lot today. Can I just shake your hand?"

"Sure," Dracula smiled. "It's always glad to meet a fan."

He clasped the man's hand warmly. Then suddenly he had a thought: "Um... you don't have a penguin tattoo, do you?"

"I do as it happens," said the man. "It's between my shoulder blades. Why?"

"Oops!" said Dracula... and he exploded.

Two men are in their flat one night watching television when they hear a knock at the door. One of them opens it to find... a vicious-looking vampire. It bares its fangs and lunges for him... but is frozen in the doorway!

"What the..." says the man, confused.

"Oh yeah, I heard about this," says his roommate. "Vampires can't enter anywhere unless they're invited. We're totally safe." He sticks his tongue out at the vampire. It desperately tries to run towards him but can't move any further inside, howling in frustration.

"Oh, come on in," says the man to the vampire, which immediately bursts through the previously forbidden barrier and lunges at the men.

"What the hell did you do that for?" his roommate asks. "Now he's going to kill us both!"

"Maybe he will, maybe he won't," says the man. "All I know is, he was scuffing up our welcome mat something awful."

> Why don't vampires have any reflections?
> Because they never pay their mirror
> subscription fees.

Weather

Four old women sitting out on a porch are discussing local happenings.

"Didja see them hailstones t'other day?" asked one. "As big as marbles they were, dented the hell out of my Oldsmobile."

"That's nothin'," says the second. "In 1974 I saw hail as big as Granny Smith apples. You had to run and hide indoors or you'd end up concussed on the floor."

"That's kiddy stuff, says the third. "In the '60s, hail used to be big as the head of a grizzly bear, they'd come barrelin' down and you'd have to leave the whole area for months."

The fourth and oldest woman then pipes up: "Only ever seen one hailstone. Struck the vehicle I was in, did quite a bit of damage."

"Just one hailstone?" the first woman asks. "That ain't too bad."

"Yeah, well, it was pretty bad. And they'd told us the *Titanic* was unsinkable!"

★ ★

The three most common types of clouds are altostratus, cirrocumulus, and those big grey fluffy ones that always chuck it down when you're out in the open and you left your brolly at your mate Australian Dave's house.

★ ★

The officer in charge of a military air traffic control tower is concerned about how the very high wind conditions might affect an upcoming mission, and barks an order to a subordinate. Half an hour later, a man in a white coat arrives in the tower. He gets the officer to pee in a cup, and then after testing it tells him he's free of disease and relatively healthy, though he may need to cut down on the sugary snacks otherwise he might be at risk of diabetes. After he's left, the officer yells at his subordinate: "I said I wanted a metereologist, not that I wanted to meet a urologist."

> "Were you wet when you got home last night? It was really chucking it down!"
> "I didn't get home last night. I was really chucking it down as well..."

A man goes to a trip advisor website and within minutes is connected with an online assistant trying to help him find his perfect destination.

"I want to go somewhere really sunny," he says.

"Okay, how about Ibiza?" the advisor says.

"Yuck! That place was way too touristy," the man replies.

"Okay, how about the Maldives?"

"Been there, rubbish weather."

The advisor wracks his brains. "The Seychelles? Tunisia? The Canaries?"

"Been, been and been... and none of them were sunny enough."

Frustrated, the advisor suggests, "How about the middle of the Sahara Desert then?"

"Nope," the man says. "I was there for two weeks. Nice people but still not sunny enough."

Completely exasperated, the advisor shouts, "WELL, HOW ABOUT THE SURFACE OF THE SUN THEN?!"

Silence. Then the man says, "Are you kidding me?... The drinks there are so expensive."

A man staggers into his house with torn clothes, covered in bruises. His wife runs to his side.

"You won't believe what just happened to me!" he says. "I was driving back from the bar, straight up along the highway, nobody on the road... when suddenly I got swept up into a tornado!"

"Seriously? Oh my God!"

"It was full of pieces of debris and whole trees, it was a nightmare!"

His wife is amazed. "Well, thank God you're safe. Did it damage the car?"

"Well, the tornado didn't, but then I ran over a scarecrow and a lion! And that man made of tin really scratched up the paintwork!"

★ ★

A woman runs into the front room of her residence. "I just looked outside and all I can see is snow, it's completely white!" she says, grinning. "There must be at least five feet of snow out there! And you know what that means... Snow Day! No work, just goofing off, chocolate, marshmallows and watching terrible daytime TV."

"Listen, Dr Kowalski," says a senior-looking man sitting in the room. "If you want to keep your job at the Antarctic Research Station, you really need to stop making this stupid joke every damn day."

How do you know if it's raining enough to cause a flood? I can't tell you, but I Noah man who can.

A man is walking through his town when he notices an unusual vehicle parked outside. It's covered in antennae, radar dishes and electrical equipment, and is reinforced steel throughout. He also notices a man with industrial goggles and a vest covered in pockets, jumping down from the front seat. He goes over to talk to him. "Excuse me, do you mind if I ask what you do?" he enquires.

"No problem, buddy," says the vest-wearer. "I'm a storm chaser. And this is my vehicle, Zephyr-1. We've got all the latest monitoring equipment, digital barometers, real-time biometric wind-mapping... the works."

"Really? And what's storm-chasing like?"

"No idea, buddy. I've never caught one yet."

What's the difference between a cyclone, a hurricane and a typhoon?
If you're right in the middle of one, WHO CARES!

●●●●●●● ● ●●●●●●

The eye of a storm is always calmer than what surrounds it. That said, you never want to be under the nose of a storm!

●●●●●●● ● ●●●●●●

In a dilapidated laboratory, a scientist is surprised to be visited by a man in an expensive suit. "Can you please confirm to me the nature of your research here?" the man asks.

"Alright," says the scientist. "Well, I'm trying to build a device that can control the weather! Imagine if a man steals a woman's purse, he's running along and then – BAM! – a bolt of lightning strikes! Or if an area is experiencing a terrible drought, you just flick a switch and they get as much rainfall as they need!"

"Well, I'm extremely interested," the clearly wealthy man says. "And I'm prepared to fund you to the tune of $5 billion..."

"Oh my God!"

"...provided you can get it completed by next Thursday."

The scientist sits down in shock. "Well, I... that's a lot of money... but next Thursday? I have to run tests, build prototypes, experiment and model scenarios... it's a big, big undertaking. Why does it have to be by next Thursday?"

"I'm having a barbecue."

Weddings

An insurance assessor is at a wedding reception and asks the bride, "So this is your fourth husband, is it?"

"Yes, that's right," she replies.

"Can I ask what happened to your first husband?"

"Oh, very sad, he died quite suddenly."

"Oh, I am sorry, what happened?"

"He unfortunately ate some poisoned mushrooms and passed away. The insurance paid out, of course, but it can never really compensate."

"That's terrible, what happened to the second husband?"

"Another tragic case. He also ate some poisoned mushrooms and passed away. The money didn't compensate for his loss."

By now, the assessor was very suspicious, and asked, "Did your third husband also die from ingesting poisoned mushrooms?"

"Oh no," she replied, "he died from a fractured skull!"

"My word, I'm so very sorry... How did that happen?"

"Well, he wouldn't eat the mushrooms!"

Wisdom

Before you criticise someone, walk a mile in their shoes. Then when you do criticise them, you'll be a mile away... and you'll have their shoes.

★ ★ ★ ★ ★ ★ ★ ★ ★ ★ ★ ★ ★

X-ray

A man slips at work and lands on his arm, causing him incredible pain. He thinks it's a sprain and has it bandaged, but weeks later it continues to cause him pain, so he goes to the hospital to have it scanned. On arrival, he follows the map to where he thinks he needs to go, only to find himself in a long, freezing cold, stainless steel room. Lying there on gurneys are four corpses. As he walks past, he notices the toe-tags attached to the bodies on the tables. They read: Ray Fitzgerald, Ray DeVries, Ray Lorenz and Ray Jones.

Sitting at a desk in the room is a medical technician. "Excuse me," the man says, "I'm sorry, but I thought this was the X-ray department."

"No," says the technician, "everyone makes that mistake. This is the Ex-Ray Department."

Two women are talking in a pub.

"How'd you get on with that young doctor last night?"

"Not great. I was trying to impress him, but panicked and told him I worked in the X-ray department."

"Did it work?"

"No. He saw right through me."

A woman passing through airport security puts her bag through the X-ray machine. Pretty soon she's pulled aside by the operator of the scanner and a security guard. "Ma'am, can you step this way please," the guard says.

"Oh God, is it the Uzi machine gun?" she asks.

"No, Ma'am."

"Is it all the cocaine?"

"No."

"The baby panda?"

"No."

"Is it the biological weapon, then?"

"No, Ma'am. It's that top. There's no way it'll go with those sandals."

Xylophone

The teacher entered the classroom and stood by the whiteboard. "Good morning, class," he said. "My name is Mr Johnson and today I'll be teaching you to play the xylophone." He turned to the whiteboard and started to write "Z...Y...", then he erased the letters. He tried again... "X... I..." but then crossed that out too. Finally he started again... "X... Y... E...", then he stopped, erased the whole thing and turned back to the class. "Good morning, class. My name is Mr Johnson and today I'll be teaching you to play the drum."

Yachts

Two men in a pub are talking animatedly. "Have you ever heard of Robin Knox-Johnston?" the first man asks. "Amazing bloke! In 1969 it took him only 312 days to circumnavigate the entire globe single-handedly."

"Blimey," says his companion, "I bet he'd have done it in half the time if he'd used both his hands."

Three billionaires sit out on the balcony at an exclusive club at Puerto Banús marina. One of them points at a very large yacht idling nearby. "See that?" says the first billionaire. "That's my new super-yacht. 500 foot long, 30 cabins, 2 heated pools and a bowling alley. I bought it with the change left over from when I sold my football club."

The second billionaire gives him a short nod. "Very nice. See the one behind it?" he says, indicating a vessel three times the size. "That's my new baby. Fifteen hundred feet of luxury quarters, onboard health spa, a shopping mall and a garage for my eight...no, wait... nine Rolls-Royces. I got it with the interest from my chihuahua's bank account. What about you, Boris?" he says to the third billionaire.

"Oh, I came off that dinghy there," he says casually, pointing at a small boat.

"Oh really?" says the second man with a superior sneer.

"Yes, the authorities say my yacht can't fit in the marina. Something about it blocking out the sun."

Yetis

Neil Cresswell, an experienced cryptobiologist, spent years and years in Tibet on the trail of the elusive yeti. He launched so many expeditions into the mountain that various parts of it were even named after him. Starting in his relative youth he searched high and low, using scientific equipment or tracking skills taught to him by the locals, all the while coming tantalisingly close to clues or traces but never once getting anything concrete.

In his diminishing years the long white-bearded man was sometimes mistaken for a yeti himself. But he still had no success as he trailed his rake-thin body through the snowy vortexes.

One day, however, exhausted, frost-bitten and almost starved, he came to the mouth of a cave-seeking shelter. There, sitting in the darkness sat the yeti, huge and feral but with a fierce intelligence in its eyes. "Human," it began. "I have watched you for decades as you have tracked and pursued me, and over time I have come not to fear you but to respect you. So I grant you this, in the twilight of your years. Here I am, the Migoi. What have you to say to me?"

Cresswell took a breath, and said, "Do you know Bigfoot? I've been looking for someone to introduce me."

Zebras

A man returns home with his shopping, looking aggrieved. "I don't understand it," he says. "Every time I go to the shop with the self-checkout barcode scanner, I get charged £4.35 more than I should. It's ridiculous!"

"Well, Steve," says his wife. "Might I suggest next time you don't take our pet zebra?"

A man is out walking when he sees a zebra standing at the side of the road. He runs up to it excitedly. "I've always wanted to do this!" he says, and leads the zebra up to where there is a zebra crossing. He walks the zebra across it to the other side of the road, smiling and waving to people as he goes. On the other side of the road he says, "That was brilliant! You're welcome."

The zebra turns to him and says, "Thanks, mate, but I was actually just trying to get in my car."

A man says to his friend,
"My uncle tried to cross a zebra with a dalmatian!"
"Wow, really?" his friend says.
"So was it spotty... ...stripy... or both?"
"Well, nothing happened. They're different species, obviously!"

Zombies

Two workmates are sitting at their desks. "You know, in the morning," the first one says, "I always feel like a zombie until I've had my first coffee."

His friend nods. "Yeah, I know what you mean. I always feel like a wolfman until I've had my anti-wolfman serum."

A man walks into an audition for play. The casting director looks at his resumé.

"It says here you were a zombie in Michael Jackson's 'Thriller' video."

"Yes, that's right."

"And in that *Generation Z* TV series."

"Mmm hmm," he nodded.

"And in the horror film *Look Out, An Actual Zombie*."

"Yep."

"It seems like you've played a zombie a lot."

"Yeah, it's funny," the man nods. "It's been like that ever since I got bitten by one."

A concert hall owner is getting his venue ready for a big evening when he hears a scraping sound at the door. He opens it, only for a horde of ravenous zombies to burst through, lunging at him and the other workers. Following behind them is his booking agent, smiling.

"What the hell have you done?" the owner says, fighting off two of the undead with a plank of wood.

"Well, you said you wanted the zombies," the agent said, ducking a vicious swipe.

"I meant the band, you idiot!! The band that's called The Zombies!"

"Oh."

Suddenly a loud rumbling noise begins shaking the entire venue. "What's that?" the owner shouts.

"Well," says the booking agent nervously. "Remember when you said you also wanted The Rolling Stones...."

Today, there are three types of zombies. The type that stagger at a slow speed, the type that run at a fast speed, and the type that jog at a medium speed, occasionally sipping from a water bottle and checking their Fitbit.

Three zombies have just pulled themselves out of their graves.

"Well," says the first. "Me go visit family. Me die ten years ago. Me miss brother and sister. Maybe they not happy to see me, but me not mind."

"Me visit old friend," says the second. "Me die 25 years ago. Friend probably lot older, but me still recognise him."

"Well, me die 230 years ago," said the third zombie.

"Oh," said the first zombie. "Everyone you know dead. That sad."

"Yes," said the third zombie. "So me go skiing."

A man all tattered and broken with green skin, an eyeball hanging out and his limbs distended and twisted somehow manages to stagger into a lawyer's office. The terrified lawyer regains his composure. "Can... can I help you, sir?"

"Yes. I was in my apartment building and the lift broke. Unfortunately, the other occupant turned out to be a zombie, and he bit me. Subsequently I too have become a zombie, and I want to sue the owners of the apartment for gross negligence.

"I'm sorry, sir," the lawyer says. "I'd like to help you, but you haven't got a leg to stand on."

> Two zombies are standing outside.
> One says, "UUhhhhhhhhhhAAAHHhhuuhh."
> "Shut up, Arthur," the other one says. "I'm sick of your moaning!"

A secret meeting is called at the highest level of the government. "Our nightmare scenario has happened," says one of the senior aides. "A man has spontaneously developed symptoms of ravenous cannibalistic tendencies, regenerating rotting flesh and a bite that transmits the condition to others. A condition we can only call... zombieism. This man is Patient Zero."

"Dear God," says the senior government minister. "Well, then, this man must totally isolated from society. Nobody must go near him... no family... no friends... in fact, it has to be communicated to the whole of society that this man must be completely shunned at all costs."

"That's no problem, sir," says the aide. "He's an accountant."

How can you tell a vegan zombie?
Because they mutter: "Grains... grains...."

A man walks into his doctor's surgery and sits down.

"What seems to be problem?" she asks.

"Well, over the last week or so my skin has turned pallid and begun to fall off, I've developed an aversion to light, my bones feel loose, my body has begun to rot, my corneas have clouded over with a milky lens, my hair is greasing and shedding, my lower jaw fell off and I have a constant craving to consume the flesh of humans and slash them with my now claw-like fingernails."

The doctor clicks her teeth thoughtfully. "Oh dear. Well, it sounds like you're showing all the symptoms of being a zombie!"

The man nods. "Thank goodness for that, Doc! I thought I was ill!"